Two Sermons
God's ability and The blood of Jesus

Three Experiences
1. Rev. Jno. Haime
2. Rev. Wm. Hunter
3. Rev. Robt. Wilkinson,

by

Rev. Bud Robinson

First Fruits Press
Wilmore, Kentucky
2015

Two Sermons: God's Ability and The Blood of Jesus; and, Three Experiences: 1. Rev. Jno. Haime, 2. Rev. Wm. Hunter, 3. Rev. Robt. Wilkinson by Bud Robinson

Published by First Fruits Press, © 2015
Previously Published by Pentecostal Publishing Company

ISBN: 9781621711940 (print), 9781621711889 (digital)

Digital version at
http://place.asburyseminary.edu/firstfruitsheritagematerial/91/

Robinson, Bud, 1860-1942.
    Two sermons : God's ability and The blood of Jesus : Three experiences, 1. Rev. Jno. Haime, 2. Rev. Wm. Hunter, 3. Rev. Robt. Wilkinson / by Bud Robinson.
    97 pages ; 21 cm.
    Wilmore, KY : First Fruits Press, ©2015.
    Reprint. Previously published: Louisville, KY : Pickett Publishing Co., [190-?].
    ISBN: 9781621711940 (pbk.)
    1. Evangelistic sermons. 2. God – Attributes – Sermons. 3. Jesus Christ – Blood – Sermons. 4. Atonement – Sermons. 5. Christian biography. 6. Haime, John, 1710-1784. 7. Hunter, William, 1728- 8. Wilkinson, Robert I. Title
    DS9 .R62 2015   915.69

Cover design by Wesley Wilcox

First Fruits Press
The Academic Open Press of Asbury Theological Seminary
204 N. Lexington Ave., Wilmore, KY 40390
859-858-2236
first.fruits@asburyseminary.edu
asbury.to/firstfruits

TWO SERMONS BY

EVANGELIST BUD ROBINSON,

"GOD'S ABILITY" and
"THE BLOOD OF JESUS."

❁

THREE EXPERIENCES,

1. REV. JNO. HAIME,
2. REV. WM. HUNTER,
3. REV. ROBT. WILKINSON.

❁

PRICE: CLOTH, 35c; PAPER, 15c.

PICKETT PUBLISHING CO.,
Louisville, Ky.   Greenville, Texas.
1432 Franklin St., St. Louis, Mo.

1

TO THE READER.

We call your special attention to the contents of this issue. You will find it interesting, instructive, edifying. We would appreciate: (1) Your prayers for God's blessing on it whenever read; (2) Your help in its circulation. It will be furnished at liberal rates in quantities for sale or distribution.

Also, please remember, this magazine is issued monthly, at $1.00 per year, and that back numbers are kept on sale. Among these are many exceedingly choice items, worthy of the widest circulation. Assorted lots will be sent at 12 copies for $1.00. Special rates on large orders.   PICKETT PUB. CO.,
Louisville, Ky.

EDITORIAL.

BUD ROBINSON.

Who has not heard of Bud Robinson! He is the in-imitable "Bud"—there are many Robinsons, but one Bud to the patch is all we can get in a generation. Raised in a cabin in Tennessee, his father a drunkard, brothers (six of them) all drunkards, mother a morphine user. Bud grew up untaught, uncared-for, untraveled, unknown—worst of all, unsaved. He tells us that to all intents and purposes he was a heathen.

At twenty years of age he could not read, and was a veritable slave of sin and ignorance. But he went into a revival meeting and heard of Jesus as the One who loved us enough to die for us. The story thrilled his being and broke his heart. He at once fell in love with this friend of publicans and sinners, and vowed that Jesus should have all there was of him. Wondrously saved, he set about spreading the good news. Got a Tes-tament, learned to read, prayed, praised, and was soon led out into the fulness of perfect love. God called him to preach and, conferring not with flesh and blood, he be-gan. Wonderful things have come to pass. Fields have opened, from the backwoods to the city tabernacle. Crowds come and laugh and cry, repent and are saved; consecrate and are sanctified.

He is humble, plain, loving, godly "Bud." Every-body loves him—how could they help it? He has poured out burning truth on the masses in Chicago, the crowds in St. Louis, the cultured throngs in Boston, the shouting hearers in Baltimore. Those who have never seen him have heard of him, and are waiting the first opportunity to sit under his spell-binding voice. Such as have had the pleasure of waiting on his ministry are anxious for a repetition of the privilege.

The writer has known and loved him for years—in fact, to know him is to love him. May our Father strengthen his frail body, anoint him even more fully than ever, and wondrously use him as the years go by. We are not a man-worshiper. When popularity comes in, grace frequently goes out; if pride springs up, usefulness dies. Let us all pray for this blessed man, that he may never forget the pit from which he was digged, or lean to his own understanding. The praises of man may become a snare, as has been the sad case with many holy and useful men. We all need to keep humble. What is man, but a hell-deserving sinner, rescued by the matchless grace of our Christ? We believe our dear brother will keep humble, and yet words of praise are dangerous to human clay. These reflections have naturally grown out of the kind words I found myself saying about him whom I truly love.

It is a pleasure to present our readers this month with two sermons preached by this good man in Baltimore. May they be as acceptable to the readers as to those who heard them, and be greatly used of God.

In addition to these sermons we give you, readers, a genuine touch of Christian experience, as written by two traveling preachers, at the request of Rev. John

Wesley, and published in the eighteenth century, considerably more than a hundred years ago, by the founder of Methodism. Such testimonies were numerous among the early Methodists, and are a goodly heritage to us, on whom the ends of the earth are come. May ever reader know this fulness, and every pulpit glow with the holy fire.

L. L. PICKETT.

GOD'S ABILITY TO SUPPLY OUR NEEDS.

EVANGELIST BUD ROBINSON.

"And God is able to make all grace abound toward you; that ye, always having all sufficiency in all things, may abound to every good work." II. Cor. 9 :8.

There are enough· "alls" in this Scripture for every shoe-maker in the world to have one. God stands behind everyone of them, and they are all pointed toward you. A great many people do not think He is able to supply their needs, but I believe He is, and I want to talk about the abundant supplies He has on hand. *He is "able to make all grace abound toward you; that ye, always having all sufficiency in all things, may abound to every good work."*

Now let us see if He is able to do for us exactly what is needed. The first thing we need as a lost world is the *mercy* of God. Has He a plentiful, or a meager supply? The Book tells us that He has great quantities. Peter writes to the *"elect according to the foreknowledge of God the Father, through sanctification of the Spirit, unto obedience and sprinkling of the blood of Jesus Christ; grace unto you, and peace be multiplied. Blessed be the God and Father of our Lord Jesus Christ, which according to his abundant mercy hath begotten us again unto a lively hope by the resurrection of Jesus Christ from the dead, to an inheritance incorruptible, and undefiled, and that fadeth not away, reserved in*

*heaven for you, who are kept by the power of God
through faith unto salvation ready to be revealed in the
last time."* I. Peter 1:2-5.

Notice in the third verse where he speaks of His
abundant mercy. That abundance is something like the
Atlantic ocean, or the Rocky mountains, or the prairies
in Texas. You ask, "How big are those prairies?"
Well, there's hardly any end to it. I can get in at my
door and ride hundreds and hundreds of miles and see
nothing but prairie land. And that is the way God
talks about his mercy.

Is there anything else we need? What would we do
if we had nothing else but mercy? Think what pardon
means to a world condemned? Without it what would
have become of me? So God links mercy and pardon,
and they make a fine composition. Isaiah says: *Seek
ye the Lord while he may be found; call ye upon him
while he is near. Let the wicked forsake his way, and
the unrighteous man his thoughts; and let him return
unto the Lord, and he will have mercy upon him; and
to our God, for he will abundantly pardon.* Isa. 55:6, 7.
And he goes on to say in that chapter: *For my thoughts
are not your thoughts, neither are your ways my ways,
saith the Lord. For as the heavens are higher than the
earth, so are my ways higher than your ways, and my
thoughts than your thoughts. For as the rain cometh
down, and the snow from heaven, and returneth not
thither, but watereth the earth, and maketh it bring
forth and bud; that it may give seed to the sower, and
bread to the eater: So shall my word be that goeth forth
out of my mouth; it shall not return unto me void, but*

*it shall accomplish that which I please, and it shall pros-
per in the thing whereto I sent it. For ye shall go out
with joy, and be led forth with peace; the mountains
and the hills shall break forth before you into singing,
and all the trees of the field shall clap their hands. Instead of the thorn, shall come up the fir tree, and instead
of the brier shall come up the myrtle tree; and it shall
be to the Lord for a name, for an everlasting sign that
shall not be cut off.*

Drop back to the tenth verse: *As the rain cometh
down, and the snow from heaven, and returneth not
thither, but watereth the earth and maketh it bring forth
and bud, that it may give seed to the sower, and bread
to the eater.* Here let us stop a moment and think of
the greatness of God. He has undertaken to feed this
world. The whole human family, with all the birds,
beasts, fish and insects, would all be dead in twelve
months if the Lord did not produce enough food for
them. Look at the fowls—where do they get their food?
And the people of the earth—it must take at least nine
hundred thousand loaves of bread a day to feed this
town of six hundred thousand inhabitants, and about six
hundred thousand pounds of meat. Where are you going
to get this? Where do we get the material to clothe the
whole world? Isn't our market groaning under the
weight of meat, bread and clothing produced? Where do
we get the material? God made it. There isn't a man
in the world with brains or skill enough to make one
Irish potato. Now you infidels, agnostics and skeptics
ought to butt your brains out against the wall and get out
of the way. If seed potatoes were lost to-night, there

isn't an infidel that could put the germ of life in and make one potato. God has to make it, and he can do it. He said, "Let there be light," and there was light; and he said, "Let there be potatoes," and they came rolling out from under the hills. We have a very poor conception of the ability of God. We think such men as McKinley and Bryan great men. Why, God is running the world; yes, and ten thousand other worlds bigger and greater than this.

Now, He has ABUNDANT *mercy and pardon* for a lost world, and he says he is able to make *all grace* abound toward you. Isn't he doing this? If you don't love him to-night, I beseech you as an honest man to lay down your foolishness, or quit eating his bread, sleeping on his beds, wearing his clothes, and talking about him, as you think, behind his back. He is looking at you. In Genesis we read, *Thou God seest me;* and in Hebrews 4:12, *"The Word of God is quick and powerful, and sharper than any two-edged sword, piercing even to the dividing asunder of soul and spirit, and of the joints and marrow, and is a discerner of the thoughts and intents of the heart."* Then if you will keep these two thoughts before you, you will quit sin to-night. Every sin you commit, you will have to meet somewhere, and settle for it. *Render unto Caesar the things that are Caesar's, and unto God the things that are God's.* He knows how you live, and he will show you every act of your life, and you will have to settle for it somewhere—if not here, at the Judgment, and then it will be too late to make restitution. At the great convention in Chicago, where there were a thousand conversions, men paid from a nickle to twelve hundred dollars making restitution. Boys paid a nickle to the street-car company for a stolen ride, and people paid up old debts.

Last summer, at Sunset, Texas, a converted—yes, a sanctified man, had something to straighten up. About fifteen years ago he stole a water-barrel, and he had forgotten all about it. But he went out into the woods and got down to pray when he heard a racket, and looking up, saw a water-barrel rolling down a hill at him. He said, "Lord, what's the matter with me?" and then went further down the hollow, and began to pray again, when he heard a racket like a span of horses tearing down on him, and there was that water-barrel again. Then he remembered about the barrel, and the very year he stole it, so he went and confessed it to the man and paid him the dollar it was worth and ten per cent. interest. That wasn't much, you say? No, but it took that to ease his conscience. You've got to settle here in this country. It's a heap easier to get right here, than there.

But I started out to show all God could do. Romans 5:17 we read: *If by one man's offence death reigned by one, much more they which receive abundance of grace and of the gift of righteousness shall reign in life by one, Jesus Christ.* This shows that God has *abundant grace.* And in the 20th verse, *Where sin abounded, grace did much more abound.* This shows you law and grace. The law is like an electric light to light up the city. A man is wandering in darkness, and doesn't know where he is. Suddenly he comes to an electric light, and it shows him not only what part of the city he is in, but also the mud and filth of the streets. But if he is going wrong, the

light has no power to stop him and send him back, or to
clean up the mud and filth; but it shines on, and locates
it. Just so, the law can locate you and show you where
you are; but grace must come in and do the rest. He
turned on the law to show us the exceeding sinfulness
of sin, and the exceeding riches of grace. That is a beautiful thought that where sin abounded grace did much
more abound. There is more grace than sin. The plas-
ter is bigger than the sore. The supply is greater than
the demand. If there is a piece of sin as big as your
hand, he has a piece of grace as big as a bed-quilt to cover
it. Or if there is a spot on your community as big as a
mud-hole, he has six acres of land to cover it. So now we
see he has an abundance of mercy, pardon and grace, and
that brings us to another thought. Go to Titus 3:5,6:
Not by works of righteousness which we have done, but
according to his mercy he saved us, by the washing of
regeneration, and renewing of the Holy Ghost; which he
shed on us abundantly through Jesus Christ our Savior.
He said he would shed the Holy Ghost on us abundantly,
would cover us with him, would give us a river to swim
in, like the river in Ezekiel 47th. when he and another
fellow started out to measure the river. At first it reached their ankles, then it got up to their knees, then to
the loins; and after that it was a river he could not pass
over. God has an abundance of just such things, and
here you go around, with your soul about as big as a
teaspoon, when God can fill you up with a whole ocean.
The least particle of grace would run you over. When I
was seeking sanctification, He just came and touched me
and I had to halloa. You don't know how little you are.

I talked like it would take all God had to satisfy me.
I didn't know how great God is, and how small I was.
It seemed that he just wasted enough grace on me to save
Texas. Such great billows rolled out of the skies I
wasn't in it. I seemed like a minnow in the Atlantic.
It goes beyond the comprehension of man. The idea
of you, with your teaspoon trying to empty the Atlantic.
Don't you think he can supply you?

An abundance of the Holy Ghost—that gives you
abundant life. *The thief cometh not, but for to steal,
and to kill, and to destroy: I am come that they might
have life, and that they might have it* MORE ABUND-
ANTLY. You get life in conversion; in sanctification
you get *abundant* life. We don't know what we *have* got
when we tell people we are sanctified. It will roll on
through ceaseless ages, and will shine on and get deeper
and sweeter. What you have got is as deep as fallen humanity, and as high as heaven. It is a great thing to get
sanctified if it fixes you up like it fixed me. It fixed me
up for two worlds.

When you get sanctified you actually live in and fulfill the 36th Psalm, verses 7 and 8—*How excellent is thy
loving kindness, O God! therefore the children of men
put their trust under the shadow of thy wings. They
shall be abundantly satisfied with the fatness of thy
house; and thou shalt make them drink of the river of
thy pleasures.* This brings us under the wings of God
himself. Could you be in a better place? How
much better do you want? Under his wings—in a house
of fat things—drinking from a river of pleasure. A
river is not a creek, nor is it a spring branch. Just think

of a branch widening out and making a creek, and then being turned into a river. Think of drinking from the Mississippi river and then looking back into the hole! Why, you can't miss it. It don't say that the river is as big as the Mississippi, and it don't say it isn't. I believe it is greater. We know it is big enough for the whole world, and it reaches from Adam clear down to Bud. Aint that wonderful? Get under his wings, and into his house of fat things. That don't mean oyster soup and ice cream suppers and strawberry festivals; but where God lives, and rules, and reigns; and people are filled with a flood of divine love. That's the river of pleasure which abundantly satisfies. That is the blessing which the world is seeking to-day; but they go to the wrong house for it—they go to the devil's house. You will never be satisfied until you are led into the house of God's fat things, and drink from the river of pleasures.

But you talk about your circumstances, and say "If you had these difficulties *I* have to meet." What is a difficulty? What is an impossibility? It is not the place at which you live, nor the condition in which you live— not the outward, but the inward condition, that brings joy. In one place it says, "In Christ Jesus you are a new creature." If you have a difficulty, take the hand-spike of faith and turn him over, and you will find a gold mine underneath. On the outside of the door of heaven hangs the key of faith. Unlock the door, and you will find it like an old Tennessee cupboard, filled with all manner of good things, and you'll come out with hulls in your beard and juice on your fingers. Then, if you go up the street and meet some fellow who doesn't like you and gives you a slap, he'll get honey on his hands and go to licking it off and get under conviction and come back to see what it is you've got, anyway.

"It shall be done" and "it came to pass" are twin brothers, and "it shall be done" runs clear through the Bible. That's the meaning of this old puzzle, "If at first you don't succeed," suck till you get the seed. That is the only way things are to be done.

If your experience has juice in it, it will have teeth; and if it has teeth, it will bite; and if it bites, it will get hold of somebody; and if it gets hold of somebody, it will make him holloa; and if it makes him holloa, you can get him located and know where to work.

This leads to another passage. Jeremiah 33:6, where he is speaking of the backslidings of the people and city: *Behold, I will bring it health and cure, and I will cure them, and will reveal unto them the* ABUNDANCE OF PEACE AND TRUTH. I suspect peace and truth are the finest Christian ingredients in a man's life. *Thou wilt keep him in perfect peace, whose mind is stayed on thee.* Isa. 26:3; and *Great peace have they which love thy law; and nothing shall offend them.* Psa. 119:165. This brings us to the place where the world can't offend us, and we can in everything give thanks. You say you can't give thanks in everything. "What if I go up the street and a fellow knocks me down with a brick-bat?" Well, thank God from the depths of your soul that you didn't knock him down. If a man lies on you, it needn't offend you. The liar takes his part in hell, and not the man who is lied on. Jesus said in John 14:27, *My peace*

I leave with you; and in Phil. 4:6, 7, Paul says, *Be careful for nothing, but in everything by prayer and supplication with thanksgiving let your requests be made known unto God. And the peace of God which passeth all understanding shall keep your hearts and minds through Christ Jesus.*

The peace of God that passeth understanding. There you have got peace located. The understanding is located in the head, and peace in the heart, so you see it passes right by the understanding and hits you in the heart. You say that's not the correct rendering. Have you got anything more correct? The peace that passeth understanding runs right by your head. A man's head is nothing but a knot on the end of his back-bone, anyway. God is not after your head, but your heart, which is the seat of the affections. People would be better if they would unload their head religion and get something in their hearts.

The Word was made flesh and dwelt among us, full of grace and truth, and of his fulness have all we received, and grace for grace, for the law was given by Moses; but grace and truth came by Jesus Christ. John 1:14, 16, 17. You see, now, where we are going to land. John 8:32 says: *Ye shall know the truth, and the truth shall make you free.* And John 14:6, *Jesus saith unto him, I am the way, the truth, and the life.* Bless the Lord, he has just told you what the truth is. So when God reveals *abundance of peace and truth,* he reveals Jesus Christ, for he says *Ye shall know the truth, and the truth shall make you free;* and in John 8:36, *If the Son, therefore, shall make you free, ye shall be free indeed.* I don't know what the *indeed* means, unless it is to drive the nail through and clinch it on the other side.

Notice two other things of which God has an abundance. The first is *love*. That is the real honey out of the rock, the sweetness and juice of perfect love. It is described beautifully in Eph. 3 :14-21: *For this cause I bow my knees unto the Father of our Lord Jesus Christ, of whom the whole family in heaven and earth is named, that he would grant you, according to the riches of his glory, to be strengthened with might by his Spirit in the inner man; that Christ may dwell in your hearts by faith; that ye, being rooted and grounded in love, may be able to comprehend with all saints what is the breadth, and length, and depth, and height; and to know the love of Christ, which passeth knowledge, that ye might be filled with all the fulness of God. Now unto him that is able to do exceeding abundantly above all that we ask or think, according to the power that worketh in us, unto him be glory in the church by Christ Jesus throughout all ages, world without end. Amen.* Well, of course he had to say "Amen"—there was nothing else to say. He reached the top and couldn't go any further. He had you filled with all the fulness of God, and said he was able to do exceeding abundantly above all we ask or think. We will never be able to exhaust his love. He takes what nobody else wants. He loves to save. His great loving heart was moved with compassion for me, and he reached down his loving arms and pulled me up, and put a song in my mouth, and praises in my heart, and it has been twenty-one years, and he's never thrown up my mean kin-folks to me yet. It makes me love him, and shows him to be a God of love.

One other thing, and that brings us to a place where we are ready for heaven. Peter writes: *For so an entrance shall be ministered unto you* ABUNDANTLY *into the everlasting kingdom of our Lord and Savior Jesus Christ.* So we have AN ABUNDANT ENTRANCE. We won't hug the gate posts, but with our wedding dress on, and all its trimmings, we'll go in and run up the street probably a mile wide, swim across the river and climb the tree of life, whose fruit is as big as your fist, and ripens every month in the **year; fruit** without any peeling on it, or any seeds in it, and that will melt in your mouth.

Now, put these things together, and see if it is not worth while to trust God to supply all your needs. He has an abundance of mercy, pardon, grace, the Holy Spirit, eternal life, a house of fat things, river of pleasures, an abundance of love. and an abundant entrance into heaven.

If you have got the thing and live it, you will draw. Christ said : *I, if I be lifted up, will draw all men unto me.* I'll show you the difference between people. A man or woman comes to your house, you give him a chair, pass kind words, you open the door and he walks away, and you think but little about it. A few days after, somebody else comes. He sits down and talks, and you get close and listen. He talks about Jesus, and about your trials, and sympathizes with you. Before he leaves, he gets down and puts one arm around Jesus and the other around your family. Then he goes to the door and you go. He goes out on the porch and you follow. You walk beside him to the gate. He gets into his buggy, and you go between the hind wheel and fore wheel, and get one foot on the axle and talk. And then you shake hands, and then you stand and watch him till he gets out of sight, and say, "Well, I do love John." What's the difference between these two fellows? One drew, and the other didn't. I've had such people come to my house. They know what Paul meant by being "all things to all men." That's what I mean by saying, when I see an Indian, I want to be an Indian, with long, coarse, black hair and cheek bones standing up high; or when I'm preaching to the negroes, and they begin to groan and exclaim, "Dat's so, boss!" or cry out, "Lawd, help dis nigger!" and go to shouting, or off in a trance— I look at them and say, "Lord, if I can be a better man by being a negro, kink my hair and flatten my nose out all over my face, and paint my skin black." So our God, by reaching the high and low, brings down the high, and brings up the low, and puts them on the same level, and gives them an inheritance to a home in the clouds.

I am glad he is my Savior, and I can recommend him to you.

THE BLOOD OF JESUS CHRIST.

BY REV. BUD ROBINSON.

The Lamb slain from the foundation of the world.
—Rev. 3:18.

I want you to pray while I talk to you awhile on the Blood of Jesus Christ, our only hope of heaven. Back behind our redemption is the blood of Jesus. In the ninth chapter of Hebrews, verses 11-22, we read:

But Christ being come a high priest of good things to come, by a greater and more perfect tabernacle, not made with hands, that is to say, not of this building; neither by the blood of goats and calves, but by his own blood he entered in once into the holy place, having obtained eternal redemption for us. For if the blood of bulls and of goats, and the ashes of a heifer sprinkling the unclean, sanctifieth to the purifying of the flesh, how much more shall the blood of Christ who, through the Eternal Spirit offered himself without spot to God, purge your conscience from dead works to serve the living God? And for this cause he is the mediator of the New Testament, that by means of death, for the redemption of the transgressions that were under the first testament, they which are called might receive the promise of eternal inheritance. For where a testament is, there must also of necessity be the death of the testator. For a testament is of force after men are dead; otherwise it is of no

20

strength at all while the testator liveth. Whereupon neither the first testament was dedicated without blood. For when Moses had spoken every precept to all the people according to the law, he took the blood of calves and of goats, with water, and scarlet wool, and hyssop, and sprinkled both the book and all the people, saying, This is the blood of the testament which God hath enjoined unto you. Moreover, he sprinkled likewise with blood both the tabernacle and all the vessels of the ministry. And almost all things are by the law purged with blood; and without shedding of blood is no remission.

Notice the last verse—*Without shedding of blood is no remission.* This is a picture, of course, of the blood of Christ, a real atonement. Without it, we are helpless, lost. I have heard it said that we don't need the *blood;* that what we need is the *life* of Christ; that there is no reason why he should have died, because we need his life. Remember, *Without blood there is no remission.*

In Rev. 3:18 you will find my text: *The Lamb slain from the foundation of the world.* Seven hundred and twelve years before this, Isaiah saw Him as a "Lamb led to the slaughter." And in 1. Peter 1:18, 19, we read: *Forasmuch as ye know that ye were not redeemed with corruptible things, as silver and gold, from your vain conversation received by tradition from your fathers; but with the precious blood of Christ, as of a lamb without blemish and without spot.*

Brother, it gives me more comfort than everything else in the world, to know that while the Father loved me, the Son was willing to die for me. God was willing to rob heaven of its brightest jewel, and Jesus was wil-

ling to get into the human family to redeem it. Paul, in
writing to Timothy, said: *Without controversy, great is
the mystery of godliness: God was manifest in the flesh,
justified in the Spirit, seen of angels, preached unto the
Gentiles, believed on in the world, received up into glory.*
This is a picture of the Son of God getting on a level
with the human family. He found us in a world of
darkness, and he became our Light. He found us in the
lowest depths of poverty, and though he was rich, yet he
became poor for our sake. He found us starving to
death, and so he became the Bread of Life. He saw us
without the water of life, so *in the last, the great day of
the feast, Jesus stood and cried, saying, If any man
thirst, let him come unto me and drink.* John 7:37. He
found us weary, guilty, heavy-laden, and said, *Come unto
me, all ye that labor and are heavy-laden, and I will give
you rest.* Matt. 11:28.

Well, what did we have? Nothing. And when I was
condemned to die, he ran to my rescue, and through his
blood I have redemption.

This is God getting on a level with us. He had
never been on a level with us before, not till Jesus was
manifest in the flesh. He had sat on the throne, and
people had bowed to him as the God of the universe. But
when Jesus was manifest in the flesh, that was God the
Father getting on a level with us, God in Christ reconcil-
ing the world to himself. Now, God had never been on
our level before, because he had never been without a
home, till Jesus came in the flesh and could say: *Foxes
have holes, and birds of the air have nests, but the Son
of man hath not where to lay his head.* Luke 9:58. He

had seen men walking this earth without a home, but he did not know how to sympathize till he laid aside his robes and took upon himself, not the nature of angels, but the seed of humanity. He had never before been without friends. The whole earth had taken off their hats to him as God Almighty; but when he came as Jesus the Christ, all men forsook him and fled, and he had no friends. This was getting on a level with you and me. He had never been poor, and so couldn't sympathize with the poor man. But he said he would put on the human form, and be just like one of the boys, and we knew how to treat him then. He had seen many in prison, and tied up to the stake, but he had never taken a whipping. We can't conceive of God at the whipping-post. But we whipped him when he came to stay with us; and *by his stripes we are healed* (Isa. 53:5). God had never paid taxes. He created the heaven and the earth. But when he put on the human, they made him pay taxes.

When we think of God Almighty getting on a level with us, why don't we love him better? Why do we turn up our noses and walk off? Lord, help me to be thankful that he is willing to get his shoulder to mine and help me carry my burden. *Forasmuch as we know that we are not redeemed with corruptible things, but by the precious blood of Christ.* ——

Another text in Ephesians 1:7 is, *In whom we have redemption through his blood, the forgiveness of sins, according to the riches of his grace.* With the forgiveness of sins is redemption. It is proved beyond a doubt that without the shedding of blood we could not have been pardoned.

Then through his blood we are justified. But some-one says, "I thought it was by faith." Well, it is by the blood of Christ. You have got to exercise faith, and you have got to exercise it yourself. Some people have been waiting years and years for God to put faith in them. If the Lord should put faith in you, you couldn't do any-thing with it. Turn the thing around and put your faith in him, and when you do, it reaches him. There are men and women who have been living with their unsaved wives and husbands and children for years, and have been waiting for God to put faith in them for their salvation. If I had waited for that, I never would have done any-thing; but when I put my faith in God, he enabled me to put one arm around him, the other around the world, and get on a level with them.

He came as our Bread and our Water, and *He giveth his beloved sleep* (Psa. 127:2). Why, a sanctified man goes to sleep in the arms of Jesus, and the angels fan him with the breath of heaven and keep the flies off him. We sleep in the arms of Jesus because we put our faith in him. I was talking to a man at the altar the other day, who said he had been praying for twenty-one years, and God had never put the faith in him to believe. A very little faith in God will make the billows of glory roll, and give you a heaven to go to heaven in. We are justified by faith on our part, and by the blood on his part. I am glad we can run back to the atonement, and that we are justified by the blood of Jesus Christ. To-night, if I knew that a million worlds bigger than this,

and every star filled with gold and silver mines was
mine, and I had to give them up, or give up God Almighty, I'd say, "Let the worlds float on." There is
nothing so precious as the blood of Jesus, that washes
and cleanses. Oh, the songs that are written on the blood
of Jesus! Hear Cowper as he sings:

"In evil long I took delight,
　　Unawed by shame or fear,
Till a new object struck my sight,
　　And stopped my wild career.

"I saw One hanging on a tree,
　　In agonies and blood,
Who fixed his languid eyes on me,
　　As near his cross I stood.

"Sure never till my latest breath
　　Can I forget that look:
It seemed to charge me with his death,
　　Though not a word he spoke.

"My conscience felt and owned the guilt,
　　And plunged me in despair;
I saw my sins his blood had spilt,
　　And helped to nail him there.

"Alas! I knew not what I did!
　　But now my tears were vain:
Where shall my trembling soul be hid?
　　For I the Lord have slain!

"A second look he gave, which said,
　　'I freely all forgive;

> This blood is for thy ransom paid;
> I die that thou mayst live.'

> "Thus, while his death my sin displays
> In all its blackest hue,
> Such is the mystery of grace,
> It seals my pardon, too."

So we are redeemed, forgiven, cleansed, sanctified, all through the blood. To have that cleansing makes a church member out of you. The church is a spiritual institution, and you are born into it, and can't join it. I heard a man say that when he was nineteen years old he was born of the Spirit, and a few days after, they voted him into the Missionary Baptist Church, and he knew that wasn't the true church, because he was born into the one, and joined the other several days after. So, when a man is converted and comes into the spiritual kingdom, he is actually bought and paid for in blood. Every hair that grows on his head, every nickel of money, every dollar that comes into his hand, actually belongs to God.

In Acts 20:28, Paul tells them to *take heed therefore unto yourselves, and to all the flock, over the which the Holy Ghost hath made you overseers, to feed the church of God, which he hath purchased with his own blood.* When you are converted, he brings you into his church, and if you are a member, you are simply his. There is the same idea in the 23d Psalm. You say, "I don't see any connection." Well, if you are the Lord's sheep, every ounce of wool you produce is his. All you do is the wool you produce. If you are the Lord's sheep, every time he wants wool, he has a right to shear you. But many of the sheep get into a cockle-burr patch, and look more like a dog than a sheep, and it is more trouble to get the burrs out than the wool is worth. But I guess they'll have to pass off for sheep, as they've got a little wool, though it's awful poor wool, full of cockle-burrs and Spanish-needles. The idea of a man actually bought by the blood of Jesus to take the reins out of God's hand and get into the slush and mud and look more like a dog than a sheep! Well, any man that gets on my back-track will find that my wool is clean. When you get into the church, you belong to him, and you fulfill the Scripture in the sixth chapter of I. Corinthians: *What! know ye not that your body is the temple of the Holy Ghost, which is in you, which ye have of God, and ye are not your own? For ye are bought with a price; therefore glorify God in your body, and in your spirit, which are God's.* Ye are bought with a price, and without it you would never see through the gate, and every man who comes to the gate, and God the Father can't see in him the image of His Son, he won't get in.

Do we need anything after we are justified? Why, then we just get to the place where God can do for us. In conversion we get out of the devil's chain-gang, and the great God puts his loving arms around you, and you have an artesian well bubbling up in you all the time. He can now take his child and make him clean. It is impossible to be baptized with the Spirit until you are born. When converted you are brought out of darkness, for he is the Light of the world. A man with a light can walk. A man that has spiritual light, goes somewhere. *If we walk in the light as he is in the light, we have fellowship one with another, and the blood of Jesus Christ cleanseth us from all sin.* I. John 1:7. **A dead man** don't walk. The blood cleanseth from *all* sin. "All" means the whole lump, and no professor can define all and make it mean a part. Then when cleansed from all sin, you are one of the elect children of God. I believe in election with all my heart. There is but one way you can be elected, and that is through the blood. *Elect according to the foreknowledge of God the Father, through sanctification of the Spirit unto obedience and sprinkling of the blood of Jesus Christ. Blessed be the God and Father of our Lord Jesus Christ, which according to his abundant mercy hath begotten us again unto a lively hope by the resurrection of Jesus Christ from the dead, to an inheritance incorruptible, and undefiled, that fadeth not away, reserved in heaven for you who are kept by the power of God through faith unto salvation ready to be revealed in the last time.* I. Peter 1:2-5. Note here, the Spirit is never given in this sense until after the blood is shed. He strives with me and I obey, and Father, Son and Holy Ghost all three vote unanimously for me, and the angels count the ballots, and they begin to shout over there, and I over here. That's the proof that I'm elected. And there is nobody to vote against me. It's the only election the devil is not allowed to vote in. You can't even elect the officers in a Sunday-school, but what he puts his finger in the pie.

We have a battle here to fight. Because I am elected, doesn't make the devil quit fighting; but there's a way to overcome, as we learn in Revelation 12:11—*They overcame by the blood of the Lamb and the word of their testimony.* When you get under the blood, you become an heir— a joint-heir—with Christ, and it is no trouble to overcome. Of course they had an experience, or they couldn't testify. The churches that discourage testimony, dry up and go to seed. They hold their protracted meetings, and it reminds me of a threshing machine, when they feed the mules and the hands, and raise the dust, and then go around to the spout, and you'll find nothing coming out. I wouldn't run a threshing machine if I couldn't get wheat. I can take you to one city with ten Methodist Episcopal churches, built at a cost of $240,000, their running expenses $13,000, and all ten in six years only received forty-nine on probation. They cost $1,691 a head. For the next eleven years, they took in no members at all. Isn't that running a church threshing machine, and feeding the mules and the hands, and getting no wheat? Let us wake up. But, you say, "*We* are sanctified, and can beat that." Well, we are not doing much. There are many who are losing ground. Some of you women have lived twelve or fifteen years with a man, and have not won him for Jesus. If a woman couldn't bring her own husband and children to Jesus, it doesn't look as if she could bring any other woman's. Let's get into the fountain and overcome by the blood of the Lamb and the word of our testimony, and go after our own families. If the holiness movement would undertake to save our own families, we would have the greatest revival that has ever been known. How the fire would fall up and down the land. Go after your own, and go after others, too. I know a number of men preaching holiness and having apparent success, and their wives and their children are unsaved, and their homes not pleasant. But of course I'm not condemning all—some can't help it. But if anybody in the world is worth saving, it is mine. If *Jesus* loved and died for mine, *I* ought somehow to get hold and pull down grace for them. I know one good man, and his wife is a perfect notch on a stick—yes, an incarnate devil. There are not many women like that. But he loves her, and he is as patient as an ox, and as sweet as honey. I love him and respect him; but I believe if he would fast and pray it wouldn't be a week till God would shake her over a burning hell; and I believe if my wife was like that, it wouldn't be a month before she was converted or in a lunatic asylum.

I believe there is not a man or woman under the sound of my voice to-night, but what, if you would think calmly of how you are wading through the blood of Jesus, in twenty-four hours you would be saved or a raving maniac. But you do not think about where you are going, or the company you will keep. The devil won't let you. Sometimes it flies like a bird over your head; but if you would sit down and think what it cost God to redeem you, you'd be saved. But if you did get to praying and earnestly seeking salvation, the devil would say, "Of course you need it, and you ought to get it after awhile; but there is no use making a fool of yourself and getting it now." I plead with a neighbor to come to Christ, and when he was dying they sent for me to come and pray with him. And while he was dying, he kept begging his wife to keep the devil off while he died, and his life went out with a wail. His wife fell and never spoke for nine hours. He said the devil had actually come after him before he was dead, and the devil had not let that man think before about eternity.

Have you ever read "Letters from Hell"? The writer describes a man who explored that country and finally came to the river of death, as black as tar—a horrible stream, coming out of that awful country of darkness. He came to a man who was stooping down and trying to wash the blood off his hands, and saying, "What is truth?" About 1900 years ago, the same man tried my Christ, and tried to wash off the stain in a little rain water. Now he is ever washing them in that stream, and saying with a wail, "What is truth? What is truth?" Look at his hands, as the blood drops out of his pores, and he's been washing for 1900 years. It didn't take him long to commit his sin, but he has the blood of Jesus Christ on his soul forever.

When I was at a camp-meetting in Gordon, Texas, there was a beautiful girl came to the meeting, and she was leaning on the arm of a fellow with a buggy whip in his hand and a cigarette in his mouth, and all they did was to laugh and make fun. I went back there in about twelve months, and she wasn't on the ground. While there the matron of a rescue home at Fort Worth wrote my wife a letter and asked us to stop off in the city. We did so. There were about twenty-five girls in the home. One day I got word to come into one of the rooms and see a girl who said she knew me. To my surprise, there lay that beautiful girl, with a four-days-old baby boy in her arms, and her parents didn't know where she was.

O, the folly of trampling on God's love. I will never forget the awful expression of her face, as great drops of perspiration stood on it, and black rings under her eyes, with no friends, no hope, and she only seventeen years of age, away from home, from mother, from God, and in sin; and just a year before she thought it the funniest thing in the world to make fun of religion.

Friends, if you have not got religion, get it! You are going to need it awfully bad.

EXPERIENCE OF REV. JOHN HAIME.

To THE REV. JOHN WESLEY.

REV. SIR.—I was born at Shaftsbury, Dorsetshire, in 1710. My father followed gardening, and brought me up to the same employment for several years, but I did not like it, and longed for some business, that would allow me more liberty. In the mean time, I was very undutiful to my parents, and much given to cursing, swearing, lying, and Sabbath-breaking. But I was not easy in this way, being often afraid, that the devil would carry me away.

I was then placed with my uncle to learn to make buttons. I liked this well at first, but was soon tired of it. However, I stayed out the year. But my uncle then removing to Blandford, I was out of business. I wrought in many places, but stayed in none, being like a troubled sea, that cannot rest. After some time I went to my uncle at Blandford, and wrought with him about a quarter of a year. But still I found no satisfaction in any thing, neither in working, eating, drinking, nor even in sleeping; though neither I myself, nor any of my acquaintances could imagine what was the matter with me.

Some time after, as I was working alone, the devil broke in upon me, with reasonings concerning the being of a God, till my senses were almost gone. He then so strongly tempted me to blaspheme God, that

I could not withstand. He then told me, "Thou art inevitably damned." And I readily believed him. For I thought, though I have not cursed God outwardly, yet he looketh to the heart. This consideration made me sink into despair, as a stone into the mighty waters.

I now began to wander about by the river side, and through woods and solitary places, many times looking up to heaven with a heart ready to break, thinking I had no part there. I thought every one happy but myself: the devil continually telling me, there was no mercy for me. Yet I thought it was hard to be banished for ever from the presence of a merciful God. I cried to him for help; but I found no relief; it seemed to be all in vain. So I said, like the men of Judah, *There is no hope;* and then gave the reins to my evil desires: not caring which end went foremost, but giving myself up again to wicked company, and all their evil ways.

If at any time I grew uneasy again, I stifled it by drinking, swearing, card-playing, lewdness, and the like works of darkness, which I then pursued with all greediness. And I was hastening on when the great tremendous God met me as a lion in the way, and his Holy Spirit, whom I had been so long grieving returned with greater force than ever. I was afraid to shut my eyes, lest I should awake in hell. I was terrified when asleep; sometimes dreaming that many devils were in the room, ready to take me away; sometimes that the world was at an end, and I was not ready to appear before the Judge of quick and dead. At other times I thought I saw the world on fire, and the wicked left to burn there-

in, with myself among them, and when I awoke, my senses were almost gone.

I was often on the point of destroying myself, and
was stopped; I know not how. Then did I weep bitterly: I moaned like a dove; I chattered like a swallow.
But I thought, though my anguish is very great, it is not
like those who are lifting up their eyes in torments.
Then, for a few moments, I felt thankfulness to God.
But still the thoughts of death and judgment followed
me close for upwards of two years, till all my bodily
strength was gone. Returning home one day, and sitting
down in a chair, my mother observing my pale look and
low voice, asked, "What is the matter with you?" But I
durst not tell her: so I turned it off.

One night as I was going to bed, I durst not lie down
without prayer. So falling upon my knees I began to
consider, "What can I pray for? I have neither the
will nor the power to do anything good." Then it darted
into my mind, "I will not pray; neither will I be behold-
en to God for mercy." I arose from my knees, without
prayer; and laid me down; but not in peace. I never
had such a night before. It was as if my very body had
been in a fire: and I had a hell in my conscience. I
was thoroughly persuaded the devil was in the room: and
I fully expected every moment, that he would be let
loose upon me. I judged myself to be one of the worst
creatures that God ever made. I thought I had sinned
beyond the reach of mercy. Yet all this time I kept to
the church, though I was often afraid to go, lest the
church or the tower should fall upon me.

In spring, I was employed by a tanner, to go with his

carriage, and fetch dried bark. As I was returning by myself, I was violently tempted to blaspheme, yea, and hate God: till at length, having a stick in my hand, I threw it towards heaven, against God, with the utmost enmity. Immediately I saw in the clear element, a creature like a Swan, but much larger, part black, part brown. It flew at me, and went just over my head. Then it went about forty yards, lighted on the ground and stood staring upon me. This was in a clear day, about twelve o'clock: I strove to pray, but could not. At length God opened my mouth. I hastened home, praying all the way, and earnestly resolving to sin no more. But I soon forgot my resolution, and multiplied my sins, as the sands on the sea-shore.

To complete all, I enlisted myself for a soldier, in the queen's regiment of dragoons. When we marched for Gloucester, on Christmas day in the morning. 1739; the thoughts of parting with all my friends, my wife, and children, were ready to break my heart. My sins likewise came all to my remembrance, and my troubles increased night and day. Nevertheless, when I became acquainted with my comrades. I soon returned as a dog to his vomit. Yet God soon renewed my good desires. I began to read, and pray, and go to church every day. But frequently I was so tempted there that it was as much as I could do, to avoid blaspheming aloud. Satan suggested, "Curse him, curse him!" perhaps an hundred times. My heart as often replied "No! No! No!" Then he suggested, "Thou hast sinned against the Holy Ghost." But I still cried unto God, though the deep

waters flowed over me, and despair closed me in on
every side.

Soon after we marched to camp at Kingsclear, in
Hampshire. Thence we removed to winter quarters at
Farringdon. I was still deeply miserable through sin;
but not conqueror over it. This was still my language,

"Here I repent, and sin again:
Now I revive, and now am slain!
Slain with the same unhappy dart,
Which Oh! too often wounds my heart!"

After this I quartered at Highworth in Wiltshire.
Among many old books which were here, I found one
entitled, "Grace abounding to the chief sinners." I
read it with the utmost attention, and found his case
nearly resembled my own. Having soon after orders to
march for Scotland, we marched the first day to Ban-
bury, where I found again, in a bookseller's shop, "Grace
abounding to the chief of sinners." I bought it, and
thought it the best book I ever saw: and again I felt
some hope of mercy. In every town where we stayed,
I went to church. But I did not hear what I wanted,
*Behold the Lamb of God, who taketh away the sin of
the world.*

Being come to Alnwick, Satan desired to have me,
that he might sift me as wheat. And the hand of the
Lord came upon me with such weight, as made me roar
for very anguish of spirit. I could truly say, *The ar-
rows of the Almighty are within me; the poison whereof
drinketh up my spirits.* Many times I stopped in the
street, afraid to go one step further, lest I should step into hell. Then I cried unto the Lord and said, "*Why hast*

thou set me as a mark? Let loose thy hand and cut me off, that I sin no more against thee. I said, *"Is thy mercy clean gone for ever? And* must I perish at the last? *Save, Lord, or I perish!"* But there was no answer. So all hope was cut off.

I now read, and fasted, and went to church, and prayed seven times a day. One day as I walked by the Tweed side, I cried out aloud, being all athirst for God, "Oh that thou wouldst hear my prayer, and let my cry come up before thee!" The Lord heard: he sent a gracious answer: he lifted me up out of the dungeon. He took away all my sorrow and fear, and filled my soul with peace and joy in the Holy Ghost. The stream glided sweetly along, and all nature seemed to rejoice with me. I was truly free; and had I had any to guide me, I need never more have come into bondage. But I was so ignorant, I thought I should know war no more. I began to be at ease in Sion, and forgot to watch and pray, till God laid his hand upon me again. I then again went mourning all the day long: till one Sunday, as I was going to Church I stood still like a condemned criminal before his judge, and said, "Lord what am I going to church for. I have nothing to bring or offer thee, but sin and a deceitful heart." I had no sooner spoke than my heart melted within me, and I tried earnestly to him for mercy, till my strength failed me, and it was with difficulty I could walk out of the room.

The next morning as I was going to water my horse, just as he entered the river, in a moment I felt the love of God flowing into my soul. Instantly all pain and sorrow fled away. No fear of hell or the devil was left;

but love to God and all mankind now filled my ravished soul. As the people with whom I quartered had often the Bible and other good books in their hands, I told them what God had done for my soul: but they understood me not. However I doubted not, but my comrade would rejoice with me, being counted a religious man. But I was disappointed again. His answer was, "Take care; for Satan can transform himself into an angel of light." Thus finding none who was able to give me any instruction or direction, I soon got into unprofitable reasonings, which damped my fervor, so that in a little time, I was again in heaviness.

Soon after I was sent with the camp equipage to London. The next day I marched for Leith. I had scarce set out. when God was pleased to reveal himself in a most comfortable manner to my soul. And my comfort increased all the day, so that I hardly knew how I went. We waited for the ship seven days. During this time I was off my watch again: so that before we sailed. I was weak, and like another man. For two days we had pleasant weather: but on the third the wind suddenly rose, attended with furious rain. The seas frequently covered the ship, and in the midst of our distress, broke in to the main hatches. I was not (as Jonah) *asleep in the sides of the ship,* but was just at my wits end. I prayed with many tears, expecting every moment the sea to be my grave. I was grieved, that I had so abused the goodness of God, and troubled beyond expression. The storm lasted two days and two nights: then God was pleased to still the winds and seas.

At our arrival in London I was somewhat refreshed

in spirit, being truly thankful that I was out of hell. But I was soon in the depth of despair again, afraid of dropping into hell every moment. Soon after I went to hear Mr. Cennick, (then one of Mr. Whitefield's preachers) at Deptford. Coming back, I told him the distress of my soul. He said, "the work of the devil is upon you," and rode away! It was the tender mercies of God, that I did not put an end to my life. I cried, O Lord, my punishment is greater than I can bear!

Yet I thought, if I must be damned myself, I will do what I can that others may be saved. So I began to reprove open sin; whenever I saw or heard it, and to warn the ungodly, that if they did not repent, they would surely perish. But if I found any that were weary and heavy laden, I told them to wait upon the Lord, and he would renew their strength. Yet I found no strength myself, till reading one day in what manner God manifested himself to Mr. Cennick, I cried out, "Lord, if there be any mercy for me, reveal it to me!" I was answered by so strong an impression on my heart, as left me without a doubt, "I have loved thee with an everlasting love." Immediately my soul melted within me, and I was filled with joy unspeakable.

Having joined my regiment again, we marched to Colchester. Here I found much peace and communion with God, which humbled me to the dust. Our next remove was to Frentford, where I had the happiness of hearing Mr. Charles Wesley preach. When the service was over I had a great desire of speaking to him, but knew not how to be so bold. Yet taking courage, I ventured to tell him my situation of mind. He gave me

much encouragement, and bade me go on and not fear,
neither be dismayed at any temptation. His words sunk
deep, and were a great blessing to me for several years
after.

Soon after we had an order to march for Flanders.
This threw me into fresh reasoning. The thought of
leaving my country, and the dangers ensuing by sea and
by land, sat heavy upon my spirit. I soon lost my peace,
yea, and my hope too. I knew I had *tasted of the good
word, and of the powers of the world to come.* Yet this
gave me no comfort. Nay, it aggravated my sorrow, to
think of losing all that God had done for me. But the
more I struggled the deeper I sunk, till I was quite
swallowed up of sorrow. And though I called upon God,
yea, with strong cries and tears, yet for a long time I had
no comfortable answer.

For a long time I was so dejected and confused, that
I had no heart to keep a regular account of anything.
I was in this state when we embarked for Flanders, in
June 1742, and as long as we stayed there. It was on
February the 18th, 1743, that we began our march from
Ghent to Germany. When I came to my quarters, my
heart was ready to break, thinking I was upon the very
brink of hell. We halted six days, and then marched
again. The day following, as soon as I had mounted my
horse, the love of God was shed abroad in my heart. I
knew God for Christ's sake, had forgiven all my sins,
and felt, *where the Spirit of the Lord is, there is liberty.*
This I enjoyed about three weeks, but then lost it, by
grieving the Holy Spirit of God. I then walked about,
much cast down, and knew not what to do. But April

22, the Lord shewed me, that I did **not live as became**
the gospel of Christ. I was greatly ashamed before God.
In the evening as I was walking in the fields with an
heavy heart, I prayed earnestly to God, that he would
smite the rock, and cause the waters to flow. He answered my prayer. My head was as waters, and my eyes
as a fountain of tears. I wept: I sung. I had such a
sense of the love of God, as surpasses all description.
Well might Solomon say, *Love is strong as death.* Now
I saw, I had *a right to the tree of life*: and knew, if I
then put off the body, I should enter into life eternal.

Feeling I wanted help both from God and man, I
wrote to Mr. Wesley: who sent me a speedy answer, as
follows:

"It is a great blessing whereof God has already made
you a partaker: but if you continue waiting upon him
you shall see greater things than these. This is only
the beginning of the kingdom of heaven which he will
set up in your heart. There is yet behind, the fulness
of the mind that was in Christ, righteousness, peace.
and joy in the Holy Ghost. It is but a little thing that
men should be against you, while you know God is on
your side. If he gives you any companion in the narrow
way, it is well; and it is well if he does not. So much the
more will he teach, and strengthen you by himself: he
will instruct you in the secret of your heart. And by and
by, he will raise up, as it were, out of the dust, those who
shall say. "Come and let us magnify his name together."
But by all means miss no opportunity. Speak and spare
not; declare what God has done for your soul: regard
not worldly prudence. Be not ashamed of Christ, or of

his word, or of his work, of of his servants. Speak the truth in love; even in the midst of a crooked generation; and all things shall work together for good, until the work of God is perfect in your soul."

We now marched on through a pleasant country; and my soul was full of peace. I did speak, and spare not, with little interruption. Only at one time, when I was speaking of the goodness of God, one of our officers, (and one that was accounted a very religious man!) told me, "I deserved to be cut in pieces, and to be given to the devil." But I was enabled (blessed be God!) to love, pity, and pray for him.

After a long and tiresome march, we arrived at Dettingen. Here we lay in camp for some time, very near the French: only the river Mayne ran between us. June 16. I was ordered out on the grand guard with all expedition. When we came to the place appointed, I saw many of the French army marching on the other side the river. It was not long before I heard the report of a French cannon. I said, "We shall have a battle to-day;" but my comrades did not believe me. Presently I heard another, and then a third; the ball came along by us. Many of the French had crossed the river, and many more were in full march toward it. We had orders to return with all speed. The firing increased very fast: and several were killed or wounded, some by the cannon balls, some by the limbs of the trees which the balls cut off. Meantime we marched on one side of the river; part of the French army on the other. The battle was soon joined with small arms, as well as cannon, on both sides. It was very bloody; thousands on each side were sent to their long home. I had no sooner joined the **regiment** than my left hand man was shot dead. I cried to God and said, *In thee have I trusted, let me never be confounded!* My heart was filled with love, peace, and joy, more than tongue can express. I was in a new world. I could truly say. *Unto you that believe he is precious.* I stood the fire of the enemy seven hours. And when the battle was over, I was sent out with a party of men to find the baggage-wagons, but returned without success. In the mean while the army was gone, and I knew not which way. I went to the field where the battle was fought; but such a scene of human misery did I never behold! It was enough to melt the most obdurate heart. I knew not now which way to take, being afraid of falling into the hands of the enemy. But as it began to rain hard, I set out. though not knowing where to go; till hearing the beat of a drum, I went toward it. and soon rejoined the army. But I could not find the tent to which I belonged, nor persuade them to take me in at any other. So being very wet and much fatigued. I wrapt me up in my cloak, and lay down and fell asleep. And though it still rained hard upon me, and the water ran under me, I had as sweet a night's rest as ever I had in my life.

We had now to return from Germany to Flanders to take up our winter quarters. In our march we were some time near the river Mayne. twenty miles from the field of battle. We saw the dead men lie in the river, and on the bank. Many of the French, attempting to pass the river, after we had broken down the bridge, were drowned, and many cast upon the banks, where there was none to bury them.

Being in Ghent, I went one Sunday morning to the English Church at the usual time. But neither minister nor people came. As I was walking in the church, two men belonging to the train came in, John Evans and Pitman Stag. One of them said, "The people are long in coming." I said, "Yet they think however they live, of going to heaven when they die. But most of them I fear, will be sadly disappointed." They stared at me, and asked what I meant? I told them, "Nothing unholy can dwell with a holy God." We had a little more talk, and appointed to meet in the evening. I found John Evans a strict Pharisee, *doing justly,* and *loving mercy,* but knowing nothing of walking humbly with his God. But the cry of Pitman Stag was, *God be merciful to me a sinner!* We took a room without delay, and met every night to pray, and read the Holy Scriptures. In a little time we were as speckled birds, as *men wondered at.* But some began to listen under the window, and soon after desired to meet with us. Our meetings were soon sweeter than our food : and I found therein such an enlargement of soul, and such an increase in spiritual knowledge, that I resolved to go, come life, come death.

We had now twelve joined together; several of whom had already found peace with God; the others were earnestly following after it: and it was not long before they attained. Hereby new love and zeal were kindled in us all: and although Satan assaulted us in various ways, yet were we enabled to discern all his wiles, and to withstand all his power. Several of them are now

safely landed on the blissful shore of a glorious immor-
tality; where, as a weather-beaten bark, worn out with
storms, may I at last happily arrive, and find the children whom God has been graciously pleased to give me,
through the word of his power!

One night, after our meeting, I told the people we
should have the room full before we left the city. We
soon increased to about twenty members. And love increased so, that shame and fear vanished away. Our
singing was heard afar off, and we regarded not those
who made no account of our labors. Such was the increase of our faith, love, and joy in the Holy Ghost, that
we had no barren meetings. Such our love to each other,
that even the sight of each other filled our hearts with divine consolation. And as love increased among us, so did
convictions among others; and in a little time we had a
society. So that now (as I had told them before) the
room was too small to hold the people.

May 1, 1744, we marched from Ghent, and encamped
near Brussels. Our camp lay on the side of a hill: we
set up our standing on a hill just opposite. We were
easily heard by the soldiers in the camp, who soon began
to *fly as a cloud,* and *as doves to the windows.* Here I
gathered together my scattered sheep and lambs. They
were the joy of my heart, and I trust to find them again,
among that *great multitude that no man can number.*
Oh what a work did God put into my hands! And who
is sufficient for these things? But God had given me such
faith, that had I continued steadfast in the grace of God,
neither things present, nor things to come, nor any crea-

ture, could have hindered my growing in the knowledge of Jesus Christ, unto my dying hour.

I took great delight in the eleventh chapter to the Hebrews. I read it over and over, and prayed much for faith. This was first in the day, and last at night in my mind: and I had no more doubt of the promises contained therein, than if God had called to me from heaven, and said, "This is my word, and it shall stand for ever." When I began preaching, I did not understand one text in the Bible, so as to speak from it in (what is called) a regular manner, yet I never wanted either matter or words. So hath God in all ages, *chosen the weak things of the world to confound the things that are mighty.* I usually had a thousand hearers, officers, common soldiers and others. Was there ever so great a work before, in so abandoned an army! But we can only say, there is nothing too hard for God! He worketh what, and by whom he pleaseth.

I was now put to a stand. I had so much duty to do, the society to take care of, and to preach four or five times a day, that it was more than I could well perform. But God soon took care for this also. I looked for no favor from man: I wanted nothing from man: I feared nothing: God so increased my love and zeal. Light and heat filled my soul, and it was my meat and drink to do the will of my heavenly Father. I cried earnestly to him, to clear my way, and remove all hinderances. Glory be to his name, he did so: for two years after this time, I was entirely at my liberty. I found means of hiring others to do my duty, which proved an unspeakable advantage. The work was great before; but we soon found a greater increase of it than ever. If Christianity consists in love and obedience to God, and love to all men, friends and enemies, we had now got a Christian society; we had the good land in possession. But this was not enough: still there was as earnest a cry in our souls, for all the mind which was in Christ, as there was in David, for *the water of the well of·Bethlehem.*

Our general method was, as soon as we were settled in any camp, to build a Tabernacle, containing two, three, or four rooms, as we saw convenient. One day, three officers came to see our chapel, as they called it. They asked many questions: one in particular asked me, what I preached? I answered, "I preach against swearing, whoring, and drunkenness, and exhort men to repent of all their sins, that they may not perish." He began swearing horribly, and said, if it was in his power, he would have me whipped to death. I told him, "Sir, you have a commission over men: but I have a commission from God, to tell you, you must either repent of your sins, or perish everlastingly." He went away, and I went on, being never better than when I was preaching or at prayer. For the Lord gave such a blessing to his word, that I thought every discourse lost, under which no one was either convinced or converted to God.

We had now three hundred in the society, and six preachers, besides myself. It was therefore no wonder, that many of the officers and chaplains endeavored to stop the work. But it was altogether lost labor: he that sitteth in heaven laughed them to scorn. And I doubt not, but he would have given me strength to have suffered death, rather than have given them up.

It was reported by many, that I was utterly dis-
tracted. Others endeavored to incense the Field Mar-
shall against me. I was examined several times, but,
blessed be God, he *stood by me,* and encouraged me to
go on, *to speak* and *not hold my peace;* neither did he
suffer any *man to set upon me to hurt me.* And so great
was my love and joy in believing, that it carried me
above all those things, which would otherwise have been
grievous to flesh and blood, so that all was pleasant to
me:

> "The winter's night, and summer's day,
> Fled imperceptibly away."

I frequently walked between twenty and thirty miles
a day; and preached five and thirty times in the space of
seven days. So great was my love to God, and to the
souls which he hath purchased with his own blood.
Many times have I forgotten to take any refreshment
for ten hours together. I had at this time three armies
against me; the French army, the wicked English army,
and an army of devils. But I feared them not; for my
life was *hid with Christ in God.* He supported me
through all: and, I trust, will be my God and my guide
even unto death.

While the work of God thus flourished among the
English, he visited also the Hanoverian army. A few of
them began to meet together; and their numeber daily
increased. But they were quickly ordered to meet no
more. They were very unwilling to desist. But some
of them being severely punished, the rest did not dare to

disobey. It is clear, the devil and the world will suffer a man to be anything, but a real Christian!

My present comrade was an extremely wicked man. He came home one day, cursing and swearing, that he had lost his money; he searched for it, and aftter some time found it. He threw it on the table and said, "There is my ducat: but no thanks to God, any more than to the devil." I wrote down the words, and complained to our commanding officer. After a few days he was tried by a court-martial. The officer asked what I had to say against him? I gave him the words in writing. When he had read them, he asked me if I was not ashamed to take account of such matters as this? I answered, "No Sir: If I had heard such words spoken against his majesty king George, would not you have counted me a villian if I had concealed them?" His mouth was stopped, and the man cried for pardon. The captain told him he was worthy of death, by the law of God and man: and asked me, "What I desired to have done?" I answered, I desire only to be parted from him, and I hoped he would repent. Orders were given that we should be parted. This also was a matter of great thankfullness.

From camp we removed to our winter quarters at Bruges. Here we had a lively society: but our preaching-room was far too small to contain the congregation. There was a very spacious place appointed for the public worship of our army, commonly called the English Church. General Sinclair was now our commanding officer. I went to his house and begged leave to speak to him. He told me, if I had business with him, I should have sent my captain, and not come to him myself. I told him, I had the liberty to speak to the Duke of Cumberland. He then asked me what I wanted? I said, "Please your honour, I come to beg a great favour; that I may have the use of the English Church to pray in, and exhort my comrades to flee from the wrath to come." He was very angry, and told me, I should not preach or pray any where but in the barracks. He asked, "But how came you to preach?" I said, "The Spirit of God constrains me to call my fellow-sinners to repentance." He said, "Then you must restrain that Spirit." I told him, "I would die first." He said, "You are in my hand," and turned away in a great rage.

I cried to the Lord for more faith, that I might never deny him, whatsoever I was called to suffer; but might own him before men and devils: and very soon after, God removed this hindrance out of the way; General Sinclair was removed from Bruges, and General Ponsonby took his place. I went to his house, and was without difficulty admitted to his presence. Upon his asking what I wanted, I said, "I come to beg your honor will grant us the use of the English Church, that we may meet together and worship God." He asked, "What religion are you of?" I answered, "Of the Church of England." Then, said he, "You shall have it." I went to the clerk for the keys; but he said, "The chaplains forbade it, and I should not have them." The general then gave me an order under his hand. So they were delivered. I fixed up advertisements in several parts of the town, "Preaching every day at two o'clock, in the English Church." And we had every day a numerous congregation, both of soldiers and townsfolk.

We had some good singers among us, and one, in particular, who was a master of music. It pleased God to make this one great means of drawing many to hear his word. One Sunday the clerk gave out a psalm. It was sung in a hymn tune; and sung so well that the officers and their wives were quite delighted with it. The society then agreed to go all together to church every Sunday. On the next Sunday we began. And when the clerk gave out the first line of the psalm, one of us set the tune and the rest followed him. It was a resemblance of heaven upon earth. Such a company of Christian soldiers singing together, with the spirit and the understanding also, gave such life to the ordinance, that none but the most vicious and abandoned could remain entirely unaffected.

The spring following we took the field again : and on May 11, 1745. we had a full trial of our faith, at Fontenoy. Some days before, one of our brethren standing at his tent door, broke out into raptures of joy, knowing his departure was at hand; and when he went into the battle declared, "I am going to rest in the bosom of Jesus." Indeed this day God was pleased to prove our little flock, and to show them his mighty power. They showed such courage and boldness in the fight, as made the officers, as well as soldiers, amazed. When wounded, some cried out, "I am going to my beloved." Others, "Come, Lord Jesus; come quickly." And many that were not wounded earnestly desired *to be dissolved and to be with Christ.* When W. Clements had his arm broke by a musket-ball, they would have carried him out of the battle. But he said, "No, I have an

arm left to hold my sword: I will not go yet." When a
second shot broke his other arm, he said, "I am as happy
as I can be out of paradise." John Evans having both
his legs taken off by a cannon ball, was laid across a cannon to die: where, as long as he could speak, he was
praising God and blessing him with joyful lips.

For my own part, I stood the hottest fire of the enemy for above seven hours. But I told my comrades,
"The French have no ball made that will kill me this
day." After about seven hours, a cannon ball killed my
horse under me. An officer cried out aloud, "Haime!
where is your God now?" I answered, "Sir, he is here
with me; and he will bring me out of this battle." Presently a cannon-ball took off his head. My horse fell upon me, and some cried out, "Haime is gone!" But I replied, "He is not gone yet." I soon disengaged myself,
and walked on, praising God. I was exposed both to the
enemy and to our own horse; but that did not discourage
me at all: for I knew the God of Jacob was with me. I
had a long way to go through all our cavalry, the balls
flying on every side. And all the way, multitudes lay
bleeding, groaning, dying, or just dead. Surely I was
as in the fiery furnace; but it did not singe a hair of my
head. The hotter the battle grew, the more strength
was given me. I was as full of joy as I could contain.
As I was quitting the field, I met one of our brethren,
with a little dish in his hand, seeking water. I did not
know him at first, being covered with blood. He smiled
and said, "Brother Haime, I have got a sore wound." I
asked, "Have you got Christ in your heart?" He said,
"I have; and I have had him all this day. I have seen

many good and glorious days, with much of the power of God. But I never saw more of it than this day. Glory be to God for all his mercies!" Among the dead, there was great plenty of watches. and of gold and silver. One asked me, will not you get something? I answered, "No. I have got Christ. I will have no plunder."

But the greatest loss I sustained was that of my fellow laborers. William Clements was sent to the hospital, John Evans. brothers Bishop and Greenwood were killed in the battle. Two others, who used to speak boldly, fell into Antinomianism. So I was left alone; but I was persuaded, this also was for my good. And seeing iniquity so much abound, and the love of many waxing cold, it added wings to my devotion. And my faith grew daily, as a tree planted by the water-side.

One of those Antinomian preachers professed to be always happy, but was frequently drunk twice a day. One Sunday, when I was five or six miles off, he took an opportunity of venting his devilish opinions. One hasted after me. and begged me to return. I did so; but the mischief was done. He had convinced many, that we have nothing to do with the law, either before or after our conversion. When I came in, the people looked greatly confused: I perceived there was a great rent in the society, and after preaching and prayer, said, "You that are for the old doctrine, which you have heard from the beginning, follow me." Out of the three hundred, I lost about fifty; but the Lord soon gave me fifty more. The two Antinomians set up for themselves, until lying, drunkenness, and many other sins destroyed both preach-

ers and   people, all but   a few that came   back to their
brethren.

We had no sacrament administered in the army for
a long season.   I was greatly troubled, and complained
aloud in the open camp of the neglect.   The chaplains
were exceedingly displeased.   But the duke of Cumberland hearing of it, ordered that it should be administered every Lord's day, to one regiment or the other.

The duke hearing many complaints of me, enquired
who I was; if I did my duty: if I would fight: and if I
prayed for a blessing on the king and his arms.   They
told his royal highness, I did all this, as well as any man
in the regiment.   He asked, "Then what have you to say
against him?"   They said, "Why he prays and preaches
so much, that there is no rest for him."   Afterwards the
duke talked with me himself, and asked me many questions.   He seemed so well satisfied with my answers,
that he bade me, "Go on;" and gave out a general order,
that I might preach any where, and no man should mo-
lest me.

*   *   *   *

I had now for some years endeavored to keep a conscience void of offence, toward God and toward man: and
for near three years I had known that God for Christ's
sake had forgiven all my sins.   I had enjoyed the full
assurance of faith, which made me rejoice in all condi-
tions: wet and weary, cold and hungry, I was happy;
finding a daily increase in faith and love.   I had con-
stant communion with the Father and the Son.   It was
my delight to do his blessed will, to do good to them that
hated me, and to call all sinners, to *behold the Lamb of*

God, which taketh away the sin of the world. But Oh!
how did the mighty fall, and the weapons of war perish!
April 6. 1746, I was off my watch, and fell by a grievous temptation. It came as quick as lightning: I knew
not if I was in my senses; but I fell, and the Spirit of
God departed from me. It was a great mercy, that I did
not fall into hell. Blessed be God for that word, *If
any man sin we have an advocate with the Father, Jesus
Christ the righteous.* . But it was twenty years before I
found him to be an advocate for me with the Father
again.

My fall was both gradual and instantaneous. I first
grew negligent in watching and prayer, and in reading
the Scriptures. I then indulged myself more and more,
laying out upon my own appetite, what I before gave
to my poor brethren. I next began to indulge the lust
of the eyes, to look at and covet pleasing things, till by
little and little I became shorn of my strength, *having
left my former love.* For many years I had scrupled
buying or selling the least thing on the Lord's day. The
sixth of April was on a Sunday. That day I was sent
to Antwerp for forage: several of my comrades desired
me to buy them some things, which accordingly I did.
I had an inward check, but I over-ruled it, and quickly
after, became a prey to the enemy. Instantly my condemnation was so great that I was on the point of destroying myself: God restrained me from this, but Satan
was let loose, and followed me by day and by night. The
agony of my mind weighed down my body, and threw
me into a bloody flux. I was carried to an hospital, just

dropping into hell. But the Lord upheld me with an unseen hand, quivering over the great gulph.

Before my fall, my sight was so strong, that I could look stedfastly on the sun at noonday. But after it, I could not look a man in the face, nor bear to be in any company. Indeed I thought myself far more fit for the society of devils than of men: everything was a burden to me, and grevious to be borne. The roads, the hedges, the trees; everything seemed cursed of God. Nature appeared void of God, and in the possession of the devil. The fowls of the air and the beasts of the field, all appeared in a league against me. I had not one ray of hope, but a fearful looking for of fiery indignation. Very frequently Judas was represented to me, as hanging just before me. Had I been cut with knives from head to foot, I could not have been more sore in my flesh, than I was in my spirit. How true is it, *the spirit of man may sustain his infirmities: but a wounded spirit who can bear?*

I clearly saw the unshaken faith, the peace, joy, and love which I had cast away, and felt the return of pride, anger, self-will, and every other devilish temper. And I knew by melancholly experience, that my last state was worse than the first. I was one day drawn out into the woods, lamenting my forlorn state: and on a sudden I began to weep bitterly. From weeping, I fell to howling like a wild beast, so that the woods resounded. Yet could I say, notwithstanding my bitter cry, *My stroke is heavier than my groaning.* Nevertheless, I could not say, "Lord have mercy upon me," if I could have purchased heaven thereby.

So great was the displeasure of God against me, that he in a great measure took away the sight of my eyes. I could not see the sun for more than eight months: even in the clearest summer day, it always appeared to me like a mass of blood: at the same time I lost the use of my knees. I cannot describe what I felt. I could truly say, *Thou hast sent fire into my bones.* I was often as hot as if I was burning to death: many times I looked, to see if my clothes were not on fire. I have gone into a river to cool myself: but it was all the same. For what could quench the wrath of his indignation, that was let loose upon me?

At other times, in the midst of summer, I have been so cold, that I knew not how to bear it. All the clothes I could put on had no effect, but my flesh shivered, and my very bones quaked. God grant, reader, that thou and I may never feel, how hot or cold it is in hell.

I was afraid to pray; for I thought the die was cast, and my damnation sealed. So I thought it availed not, if all the saints upon earth, and all the angels in heaven should intercede for me. I was angry at God, angry at myself, and angry at the devil. I thought I was possessed with more devils than Mary Magdalene. I cannot remember, that I had one comfortable hope, for seven years together. Only while I was preaching to others, my distress was a little abated. But some may enquire, What could move me to preach, while I was in such a forlorn condition? They must ask of God, for I cannot tell: his ways herein are past my finding out.

In all my trials, I have, by the grace of God, invariably kept to one point, preaching *repentance towards God, and faith in our Lord Jesus Christ*: testifying that *by grace ye are saved through faith*: that *now is the day of salvation*; and that this salvation is for all; that Christ *tasted death for every man.* I always testified, that without holiness no man should see the Lord, and that if any, though ever so holy, *draw back,* they will perish everlastingly. I continually expected this would be my lot: yet after some years, I again attempted to pray. With this, Satan was not well pleased; for one day as I was walking alone, and faintly crying for mercy, suddenly such a hot blast of brimstone flashed in my face, as almost took away my breath. And presently after, as I walked along, an invisible power struck up my heels, and threw me violently upon my face.

When we came back to Holland, I had now and then a spark of hope. One Sunday I went to Church, where the Lord's supper was to be administered. I had a great desire to partake of it. But the enemy came in like a flood to hinder me, pouring in temptations of every kind. I resisted him with my might, till, through the agony of my mind, the blood gushed out of my mouth and nose. However, I was enabled to conquer, and to partake of the blessed elements. So I still waited on God in the way of his judgments, and he led me in a way I had not known.

Whatever my inward distress was, I always endeavored to appear free among the people. And it pleased God to make me fruitful in the land of my affliction. He gave me favor in their sight; and many children were born unto the Lord. Indeed, I could speak but very little Dutch, with regard to common things: but when we came to talk of the things of God I could speak a great deal. And after I had been at prayer, many have told me they could understand almost every word I said. But what was this to me? I was miserable still, having no comfortable sense of the presence and favor of God.

I had heard of an old, experienced Christian at Rotterdam. I went to see him, and found him in an upper-room, furnished like that which the Shunamite prepared for Elisha. He looked at me but did not speak one word. However, I told him a little of my experience. He looked earnestly at me, and soon began to speak, and tell me all his heart. He said, he had lived for several years in the favor and love of God, when thinking himself stronger than he was, Satan got an advantage over him. The Spirit departed from him; his strength was gone, and he knew not where to fly for refuge. For ten years, sin held him in its iron bondage, and in inexpressible anguish and despair. But one day, as he was making his complaint to God, on a sudden light broke in: sorrow fled away, and his soul was like the chariots of Aminadab. The change was so great, that he was utterly lost in wonder, love, and praise. He knew God had *created a clean heart, and renewed a right spirit within him.* And he had now lived thirty years, without one doubt of what God had wrought. This gave me considerable satisfaction: but it lasted only a short time.

When we were going for winter-quarters, into a town in Holland, I was sent thither before our troop. A gentleman sent for me, and asked, "If I knew John Haime?" I said, "I am the man." He said, "A gentlewoman in the town wants to speak with you." I went

to her house, and she bade me welcome.   After a little
conversation she asked me, "Do you believe that Christ
died for all the world?"   Upon my answering "I do;"
she replied, "I do not believe one word of it.   But as you
know he died for you, and I know he died for me, we
will only talk of his love to poor sinners."   We were soon
as well acquainted, as if we had lived together many
years, and her house became my home.   I asked how
many she had in family?   She said, seven beside herself.
I asked, "What is to become of all these, that you are
so easy about them?"   She said, "The Lord will call them
in his due time, if they belong to him."   I asked, "Shall
we pray for them?"   She said, yes: so I began that evening.   In a few days, the servant maid was cut to the
heart; next one of her sons was convinced of sin, and
soon after converted to God.   And before we left the
town, the whole family were athirst for salvation. When
the time of our marching drew near, she was in great
trouble.   But there was no help: so we took our leave of
each other, to meet no more till the morning of the resurrection.

At another time I was quartered at Meerkirk, in
Holland, at a young woman's, whose father and mother
were lately dead.   She had many cattle, some of which
died daily with the distemper: but she never murmured.
I never before met with a woman, that was so ready in
the Scriptures; I could not mention any text, but she
would readily tell the meaning of it.   So that it was no
wonder, she was thought by others, as well as by herself,
to be a prime Christian.   I was almost of the same mind
at first: but when I had narrowly observed her, I was

thoroughly convinced she was deceived, and judged it my
duty to undeceive her. I told her, "You are not born of
God, you have no living faith." She heard me with
much composure of mind; but she did not believe me. I
continued for three weeks pressing it upon her, at all
opportunities. And one evening, the Lord made a few
words which I spoke, sharper than a two-edged sword.
Conviction so fastened upon her heart, that she was soon
obliged to take her bed. She lay about seven days in
deep distress. She had then a comfortable hope: and
this strengthened her body for a few days. But then her
convictions returned so heavy, that she was obliged to
take to her bed again, in great agony of mind. The
town's people were alarmed, and ran in crowds to enquire what was the matter: "What could distress her
who had enough of this world's wealth, and was so good
a woman?" But they gave her no satisfaction. As soon
as they were gone, she immediately called for me, and
cried out, "Oh John! I shall go to hell: the devil will
carry me away." I said, "No! You shall not go to hell!
The Lord died for poor sinners." She lay in this distress about ten days, and was brought to the gates of
death. But the good Samaritan then passed by, poured
wine and oil into her wounds, and healed both soul and
body: so that she broke out, *Jehovah is my strength and
my song. He is my salvation. Come, all that fear the
Lord, and I will tell you what he hath done for my soul.*

I now thought, it would be a blessing both to herself
and her neighbors, if she would pray with them. She
agreed so to do. I commonly prayed first, and she afterwards. Sometimes she prayed half an hour together;

and often with such demonstration of the Spirit, as well
as such understanding, that the whole house seemed full
of the presence of the Lord.   At other times she wept
like a child, and said, "Lord! what is this that thou hast
done!   Thou hast sent a man from another nation, as
an instrument of saving me from ruin?   I was rich before, and increased in goods, and knew not that I was
blind and naked."   Many of her friends and neighbors
were concerned for her, but not so much as she was concerned for them, as well knowing they were seeking death
in the error of their life. This she declared to them without reserve; and the publishing this strange doctrine
spread our names far and near, not only through the
town, but through the adjacent country.   This brought
many from distant towns to see her, who usually returned blessing God for the consolation.   Some came
upwards of twenty miles in a morning.   After break-
fast, I used to pray first: and she went on.   Many of our
visitants were much affected and wept bitterly.   And
the impression did not soon wear off.   By this means
we became much acquainted with many of the Chris-
tians in Holland.   They were a free, loving people.   So
we found them: and so did many of the Methodist
soldiers: for they gave them house-room and firing freely.   And is not the promise of our Lord sure? *Whosoever
shall give unto one of these a cup of cold water only, in
the name of a disciple, shall in no wise lose his reward.*

All this time I was still buffeted with sore temptations.   I thought that I was worse than Cain: that I
had *crucified the Son of God afresh, and put him to an
open shame.*   In rough weather, it was often suggested

to me, "This is on your account! See, the earth is cursed for your sake; and it will be no better till you are in hell." I expected soon to be a prey for devils, as I was driven from all the happiness I once enjoyed. Frequently the trouble of my mind made me so weak in body, that it was with the greatest difficulty I performed my exercise. The Lord had indeed given me *a trembling heart, and failing of eyes, and sorrow of mind. And my life did hang in doubt before me, and I feared day and night, having no assurance of my life.* Often did I wish I had never been converted; often, that I had never been born. Sometimes I could not bear the sight of a good man without pain; much less be in his company. Yet I preached every day, and endeavored to appear open and free to my brethren. I encouraged them that were tempted, "Not to fear; the Lord would soon appear for himself." Meantime I continued to thunder out the terrors of the law against the ungodly: although some said I was too positive. Too positive! What? In declaring the promises and threatenings of God? Nay, if I cannot be sure of these, I will say to the Bible, as the devil did to our Lord, *What have I to do with thee?*

At one time, I cannot remember that I had any particular temptation for some weeks. Now, I thought God had forsaken me, and the devil had no need to trouble himself about me. He then set the case of Francis Spira before me, so that I sunk into black despair. Everything seemed to make against me. I could not open the Bible any where but it condemned me. I was much distressed with dreams and visions of the night. I dreamed one night, that I was in hell; another,

that I was on Mount Etna, and that on a sudden, it shook
and trembled exceedingly; and that at last, it split asunder in several places, and sunk into the burning lake, all
but that little spot on which I stood. O how thankful
I was for my preservation! And this continued for a
while, even after I awoke: but then it fled away as a
dream.

I was often violently tempted to curse, and swear,
and blaspheme, before and after, and even while I was
preaching. Sometimes when I was in the midst of the
congregation, I could hardly refrain from laughing
aloud, yea, from uttering all kinds of ribaldry and filthy
conversation. I thought, there was none that loved me
now, none that had any concern for my soul, but that
God had taken away from every body the affection
which they once had. I cried out, *I have sinned! What
shall I do unto thee, O thou preserver of men? Why hast
thou set me as a mark against thee, so that I am a burden
to myself? I said, I am the man that hath seen affliction, by the rod of his wrath.* Frequently, as I was going
to preach, the devil has set upon me as a lion, telling me
he would have me just then, so that it has thrown me
into a cold sweat. In this agony I have often caught
hold of the Bible and read, *If any man sin, we have an
Advocate with the Father, Jesus Christ the righteous.*
I have said to the enemy, "This is the word of God, and
thou canst not deny it." Hereat he would be like a man
that shrunk back from the thrust of a sword. But he
would be at me again. I again met him in the same way,
till at last, (blessed be God)! he fled from me. And
even in the midst of his sharpest assaults, God gave me

just strength enough to bear them.   He fulfilled his
word, *My grace is sufficient for thee: my strength is
made perfect in thy weakness.*   When he has strongly
suggested, just as I was going to preach, "I will have
thee at last," I have answered (sometimes with too much
anger) "I will have another out of thy hand first."   And
many, while I was myself in the deep, were truly convinced and converted to God.

When I returned to England, and was discharged
from the army, I went to Mr. Wesley and asked if he
would permit me to labor with him as a traveling-
preacher?   He was willing: so I immediately went into
a circuit.   But this was far from delivering me from
that inexpressible burden of soul, under which I still
labored.   Hence it was, that I could neither be satisfied
with preaching, nor without; and that wherever I went,
I was not able to stay long in one place; but was continually wandering to and fro. seeking rest but finding
none.   On this account many thought me very unstable,
and looked very coldly upon me, as they were wholly
unacquainted with the exercises of soul which I labored
under.   I thought if David or Peter had been living, they
would have pitied me.   But many of my friends had not
even tasted of that bread and water of affliction. which
had been my meat and drink for many years.   May they
walk so humbly and closely with God. that they may
never taste it !

After I had continued some time as a traveling-
preacher, Mr. Wesley took me to travel with him.   He
knew I was fallen from my steadfastness; but he knew
likewise how to bear with me.   And when I was absent,

he comforted me by his letters, which were a means under God, of saving me from utter despair.   One of them
was as follows:

London, June 21, 1748.

"My Dear Brother,

"Think it not strange, concerning the fiery trial,
which God hath seen good to try you with.   Indeed, the
chastisement, for the present, is not joyous but grievous;
nevertheless it will, by and by, bring forth the peaceable
fruits of righteousness.   It is good for you to be in the
fiery furnace; though the flesh be weary to bear it, you
shall be purified therein, but not consumed.   For there is
one with you,   whose form is as the Son of   God.   Oh
look up!   Take knowledge of him who spreads underneath you his everlasting arms!   Lean upon him with
the whole weight of your soul; he is yours; lay hold
upon him!

> Away let grief, and sighing flee,
> Jesus hath died for thee, for thee.

"Mercy and peace shall not forsake you.   Through
every threatening cloud look up; and wait for happy
days."

In this miserable condition I went to Shaftsbury to
see my friends, and spent several days.   When one and
another came and asked me, What news? I told them,
"Good news; Christ died to save sinners."   But it seemed to them as an idle tale; they *cared for none of these
things*.   One day being half asleep, I was, as it were,
thunder struck with an inward voice, saying, "What
dost thou here?" I cried to the Lord for mercy, and gave

notice that on the Sunday following, I would preach in a place at the end of the town, where four ways met. The town and villages round were soon alarmed, and at the time appointed, I believe there were three or four thousand people. My inward trouble seemed suspended. I got upon a wall about seven feet high, and began with prayer. I then gave out my text, *Behold the day cometh that shall burn as an oven; and all the proud, yea, and all that do wickedly, shall be as stubble: and the day that cometh shall burn them up, saith the Lord of hosts, that it shall leave them neither root nor branch.* Mal. iv. i. Surely I preached that sermon with the power of the Holy Ghost sent down from heaven. Twelve, if not fourteen, were then convinced of sin, some of whom are, I trust, long ago safely lodged in Abraham's bosom. In a few weeks, fifty persons were joined together in society. I now preached in a large room several times a week. But the people were eager to build a house, and appointed a time of meeting to consider of the means: but on the same day, I was taken up and put into prison, two men having sworn flatly against me that I had made a riot. After I had been in prison a night and part of a day, I was taken to a public house. It was soon full of people: I immediately began preaching to them, and the lions quickly became lambs. A messenger then came in, to let me know that I must appear before the mayor and aldermen. I did so. The town-clerk told me, they would not send me to Dorchester jail, if I would work a miracle. I told them, "That is done already. Many swearers and drunkards are become sober, God-fearing men." A lawyer said, "Well, if you will take my advice, you shall not go to prison." I replied, "I suppose you mean, if I will give over preaching. But that I dare not do." I was then without any more ado hurried away to Dorchester.

My body was now in prison: but that had been a thing of little consequence had not my soul remained in prison also; in the dungeon of despair. The jailor soon came and fell into conversation with me; but when I began to preach Jesus, as the only Savior of sinners, he quickly left me to preach to my fellow-prisoners. Many of these having no righteousness of their own to bring to God, were willing to hear of being saved *by grace.* So I preached to them several times while I was in prison, and they seemed greatly affected. Meantime, God raised up two Quakers at Shaftsbury, who became bound (bondsmen) for my appearance at the quarter-sessions. I had been in prison but eight days when one of these came to fetch me out, and brought money to pay the prison-fees, and all other expenses. Had I not been put in prison, it is likely some of those prisoners would never have heard the gospel. I saw, therefore, that God did all things well. Being come back, I began preaching again; and God was present with the people. I soon received a letter from a gentleman at London, bidding me employ two counsellors and an attorney, and to draw upon him for whatever money I wanted. I carried this letter to the post-master, and asked, if he was willing to let me have money upon it? He said, "Yes, as much as you please." This was soon noised about the town: so the magistrates were glad to make up the matter. And the work of God so increased, that in a little time we had eighty in society.

During my great distress of mind, I went twice into Ireland as a traveling-preacher, and in each passage over the sea, I was very near being cast away. October 27, 1751, I preached at Mountmelick. The next morning, after I had travelled about two miles, suddenly my senses failed me. I was soon insensible where I was, and where I came from. I supported myself a considerable time, by a gate in the road: as I did not know which way to go, nor what place to ask for. At length my understanding returned, and I began to weep. But what I passed through I cannot express, so unspeakable was my anguish. But the tender mercy of God supported me therein, that my spirit might not fail before him.

In the beginning of September 1766, I was living at Shaftsbury, when Mr. Wesley, passing through on his way to Cornwall, I asked, if it would be agreeable for me to be at his house in London a few days? He said, "Yes, as long as you please;" but before I set out, I received the following letter:

"St. Ives, Cornwall, Sept. 16, 1766.

"My Dear Brother,

"I think you have no need to go to London. God has, it seems, provided a place for you here. Mr. Hoskins wants a worn-out preacher to live with him, to take care of his family, and to pray with them morning and evening."

I went down. As soon as Mr. Hoskins saw me, he said, "You are welcome to stay here as long as you live."

But no sooner did I fix there, than I was, if possible, ten times worse than before. In vain I strove to make myself easy; the more I strove, the more miserable I was: not that I wanted any thing which this world can afford. But can this world satisfy a soul, that was made for God? The distress of mind soon became intolerable: it was a burden too heavy for me to bear. It seemed to me that, unless I got some relief, I must die in despair.

RELIEF AT LAST.

One day I retired into the hall, fell on my face, and cried for mercy; but got no answer. I got up and walked up and down the room, wringing my hands, and crying like to break my heart; begging of God for Christ's sake, if there was any mercy for me, to help me. And blessed be his name, all of a sudden, I found such a change through my soul and body as is past description. I was afraid I should alarm the whole house with the expressions of my joy. I had a full witness from the Spirit of God, that I should not find that bondage any more. Nor have I ever found it to this day. Glory be to God for all his mercy.

But notwithstanding this wonderful change, I had not the faith which I had once. But I found a very great alteration in reading the Scriptures. The promises to me opened more and more: and I expected to find some great thing wrought upon me all at once. But God's ways are not as our ways, nor his thoughts as our thoughts. He led me by a way I had not known. He greatly deepened his work in my soul, and drove out his enemies by little and little, till I could clearly say, "Thy will be done." The lion became a lamb, and I found the truth of that word by happy experience, *Thou wilt keep him in perfect peace, whose mind is stayed on thee!*

I now thought I would stay with Mr. Hoskins, for he was very kind to me. But I soon began to be so bound in spirit, that I could hardly pray in the family, nay, I could not ask a blessing on our food, without much hesitation and stammering. And all the comforts of life, which were then in great plenty, became altogether comfortless. Mr. Story being then in the round, I made my complaint to him. He told me, he would take my place for a month, if I would spend that time in the circuit. This I gladly undertook: and although for the space of three weeks, my coat was not once dry upon my back, yet I was warmer within, and far more comfortable, than in the warm parlor.

When Mr. Story was gone, I thought I would stay here a few days, and then travel. But the first night I was as restless as ever: so in the morning I took my leave, and in January 1767, went into the east of Cornwall. I found it was good for me to be there; my faith increased daily. And, blessed be God, I found love, and peace, and joy in the Holy Ghost, springing up in my soul. I trust God will continue them to my dying day, and then receive me to himself.

I had long been travelling in the wilderness, in *a land of deserts and pits, a land of drought and of the shadow of death.* This had been my lot for twenty years, a just judgment of the Almighty for my sin. Blessed be his name, that he did not wholly cast me off! But

I saw clearly nothing would avail, but a fresh application of the Savior's blood to my wounded soul. I had now a happy sense of this: which, with the thoughts of his forbearing with me twenty years before my conversion; his filling me with his love for three years; his dealings with me in my fallen condition, and my present deliverance; caused my soul to overflow with wonder and praise for his long-suffering goodness. I saw nothing was too hard for God! I could cast myself on the Lord Jesus! All the promises in the Scriptures were full of comfort; particularly that: *I have known thee in the furnace of affliction.* The Scriptures were all precious to my soul, as the rain to the thirsty land. And when Satan assaulted me afresh, I did not stand to reason with him, but fled to the Lord Jesus for refuge. Hereby the snare was soon broken, and I found an increase both of faith, hope, and love. I could now truly say, *The Lord is my shepherd, therefore shall I lack nothing. He maketh me to lie down in green pastures; he leadeth me beside the still waters. He restoreth my soul; he leadeth me in the paths of righteousness for his name's sake.*

It was not my intention ever to write any account of these things, had not some of my friends greatly pressed me thereto. Nevertheless I put it off from time to time, being conscious I had no talent for writing, until my peace was well nigh lost: at last I was prevailed upon to begin. I had not written many lines before I found my soul in perfect peace. I found myself likewise greatly assisted, to recollect the manifold dealings of God with me: so that I have the greatest reason to believe it is his will that I should make known, even by these instances of his goodness, that he is *long suffering, not willing that any should perish, but that all should come to repentance.* May he bless the feeble attempt to the good of many! May they learn wisdom by the things that I have suffered! And be all the glory ascribed unto Him that *sitteth on the throne, and unto the Lamb for ever!*

THE EXPERIENCE OF REV. WILLIAM HUNTER

To THE REV. JOHN WESLEY.

August 18, 1779.

REV. AND DEAR SIR.—According to your desire, I take this opportunity to write a little of the dealings of God with me; but as I have not kept any account in writing, many things have slipped my mind. I was born in Northumberland, at a little village near Placey, in the year 1728. I was put to school early, and taught to read the Scriptures from a child; but delighted most in the historical parts of them. I felt a degree of the fear of God when very young, and sweet drawings of love. But sometimes the thoughts of death were very dreadful to me, so that I felt very unhappy. I once dreamed that Satan came to me, and would have me: when I waked, I was full of fear, and prayed much that I might be delivered from him; and the impressions abode upon my mind for many days: but as I had nobody to teach me the right way of coming to Christ, these good impressions gradually wore off.

When I was about fourteen, my father being a farmer, I was put to learn all the branches of farming. My father was very severe with me, and I dreaded him very much: and yet I was often guilty of much disobedience against him: for which I have been much ashamed before the Lord. The first time you came to Placey, I,

with several of my father's family, came to hear you:
some of my brothers were much taken with you, and, I
trust, will have cause to bless God for it for ever. When
I was about sixteen, I heard Mr. Hopper; as soon as he
began to speak, his words affected me deeply, not with
terror, but with love; I had a taste of heaven; it seemed
as though I was created anew; there was a wonderful
change in my tempers and conduct; I laid aside every
thing that I thought was contrary to the will of God,
and practised all religious duties. I attended preaching
on all occasions, and felt much sweetness therein, and
love to those that I believed were devoted to God. I went
on in this way for some time, till my companions began
to take notice of me, and call me Methodist. Some of
them set upon me one Sunday, and cursed and swore
bitterly at me, telling me I was going to leave the church,
and the religion I was brought up in. This had a
strange effect upon me; I gave way to them: they prevailed upon me to go to the ale-house; there I was over-
taken by my old sins again. The Spirit of the Lord departed from me; my heart became as hard as a stone.
Darkness covered my mind again, and I was as sense-
less to the things of God, as though I had never known
any thing at all about them. I went on in this wretched state many months, living totally without God in the
world. Through the advice of a young man, I went to
hear preaching again. A great light was communicated
to my understanding by the word, and it pierced my conscience like a sword. I felt my inward parts to be very
wicked; all the sins of my life stared me in the face, and
lay as a heavy burden upon my conscience. I roared for

disquietness of heart, and wept and made supplication.
I was convinced I could not help myself, that I could not
do anything to reconcile myself to God : and I had many
fears lest the day of grace was past. Oh, the distress
of soul I went through for many months! It was as
though I had been forsaken of God, and hell was already
begun in me. But the Lord was pleased to give me
power over sin. I forsook every sinful way, and all my
sinful companions. I sought the Lord with all my
heart in all the means of grace. I attended preaching
on all occasions, and read the Scriptures with great diligence : the way of salvation, revealed therein through
Christ, was made clear to me; and I pleaded nothing but
the merits of Christ for forgiveness. I often rose in the
night to read and pray, and the language of my heart
was,

"If I ne'er find the sacred road,
I'll perish crying out for God."

I felt great love to the Methodists, especially to the
preachers, as the servants of the most high God, sent
to teach us the way of salvation. The people took notice of me, talked with me, and wished me to cast in my
lot amongst them. I did so, though I did not think myself worthy : and I bless God I have never felt a desire
to leave them since. I continued mourning after the
Lord, and, at length he heard my cry. One day, as I
remember, I was reading in a book, where the writer
was answering that objection, concerning the day of
grace being past: the Lord was pleased to send me deliverance; I found springing hope, and a sense of his

goodness. How did I admire the love of God, and the love of Jesus Christ to me? All my thoughts were swallowed up in heavenly contemplation; and I could truly say, *The Lord is my light and my salvation, whom shall I fear? Thine anger is turned away, and thou comfortest me.*

I now tried what the Spirit had wrought in me by the marks laid down in the holy scripture: and hence I found reason to believe, that I belonged to Christ, and was a child of God. I made a free-will offering of all I had, to be his for ever; and I thank Him from the ground of my heart, that I have been kept in the same mind to this day: though I have great cause to be ashamed, that I have made no better improvement, and often mourn and weep on that account. When I had thus found the goodness of God to my own soul, I could not forbear speaking of it to others; and the Lord gave me wonderful light and courage in his blessed work. He helped me to reprove sin, wherever I met with it, with humility, meekness, and much prayer: yet without fearing the face of any man, though many said I was out of my mind, yea, and wished me out of the world. The Lord enabled me to set my face as a flint, and to bear a testimony for him, wherever I went; and I was much blessed in so doing. There was a little town not far from ours, where I sometimes went, got a few poor people together, and talked to them about their souls. I often read the scriptures to them, and sometimes made some remarks thereon. The Lord was pleased to bless my weak endeavors among them; so that a few of them gathered together, and the preacher joined them in a society, and put me in to be the leader. I met with many trials in this little way, and was often tempted to give it up; but I durst not.

I used to travel far on the Lord's day, to hear the word of God. If it happened the preacher did not come, I was pressed upon to give an exhortation to the people. This I frequently did, but I often went home distressed to the last degree, through a deep sense of my own unworthiness: yet it was not always so. At other times I was happy and lively, having strong evidence that I was doing the will of God. Meantime several of the preachers spoke to me about travelling; but the importance of the work made me afraid: till in the year 1767, at the London conference, Mr. Rowel recommended me, and I was taken in upon trial. I was then appointed for the Barnard-Castle circuit, and entered upon my work with great fear; there seemed many difficulties in my way: however, I gave myself up to the Lord, and he was pleased to give me favor in the eyes of the people.

Two years after, I was stationed in Yarm circuit. I was afterwards appointed to Barnard-Castle circuit again, and God was pleased to bless my labors, with that of the other preachers. We had such a work of God in several parts of this circuit as I never saw. Hardly any thing of the kind in England hath exceeded it, both with regard to its swiftness and depth; the power of God bore all down before it, and it seemed as if God was about to convert all the world. After I left this circuit, I was placed at Hull, then at York, and afterwards in the Scarborough circuit. We had a gracious increase of the work of God here; and I never found more enlargement of heart. We broke up much fresh ground, took in many new places, and many souls were converted to God. The last year you appointed me for the Thirsk circuit. This has been a year of trial, but the Lord has stood by me, and I am strengthened.

What success I may have for time to come. I cannot tell. It is still my one desire to give myself wholly to the Lord, and to his blessed work. I wish to live to better purpose than I have yet done, to be more fruitful in his house, and in the world. I am conscious of many defects in myself, and feel my need of Christ every moment. My soul hangs upon him, and I experience salvation from day to day: and I trust, he that has kept me till now will keep me to the end.

Wishing you all peace and prosperity, I remain,

Rev. and dear Sir,

Your affectionate son

in the Gospel of Christ,

WILLIAM HUNTER.

POSTSCRIPT.

Richmond, August 29, 1779.

Concerning the account I gave you at London, as I wrote it in haste. I believe it is very imperfect; several things have occurred to my mind since, which I should have put in, if I had then remembered them.

As touching that great salvation, being saved from inbred sin. I shall simply relate what I know of the dealings of God with me in this respect. For some time after I knew the goodness of God to my soul. I was very happy; I sung in his ways for joy of heart, and his consola-

tions were not small in me. I thought, indeed, I should
learn war no more. It was then

> I rode on the sky,
> Freely justified I,
> Nor envied Elijah his seat:
> My soul mounted higher,
> In a chariot of fire,
> And the moon it was under my feet:

> Jesus all the day long,
> Was my joy and my song,
> O that all his salvation may see!
> He hath lov'd me, I cried,
> He hath suffer'd and died,
> To redeem such a rebel as me.

But afterwards it pleased infinite wisdom to open a
new scene to me: I began to be exercised with many un-
common temptations, and felt my own heart ready to
comply with the same: this brought me into great straits,
and I began to call in question the work of grace in my
soul. O, the pain and anguish I felt for weeks together! Yet all this while I was very earnest with the
Lord; my soul clave to him, and I often said, *Though
he slay me, yet I will trust in him.* Under this exercise
I learned several things: As first, that my nature was
not so much changed as I thought: I found many
things in me which opposed the grace of God; so that
without continual watching and prayer, I was capable
of committing the very same sins which I had been
guilty of before. 2. I began to be more acquainted with

Satan's devices, and found power from God to resist them. 3. I had very affecting views of Christ, as my great high-priest, who was touched with a feeling of all my infirmities. 4. The Scriptures were precious to me, and I found great comfort in reading them. And, lastly, I was conscious of the need of a far greater change in my nature than I had yet experienced; but I then read mostly the Calvinists' writings, who all write, that sin must be in believers till death: yet I found my mind at times deeply engaged in prayer to be saved from all sin. Thus I went on for a long time, sometimes up and sometimes down, till it pleased God to bring me to hear you at Newcastle. You preached, I well remember, from the first epistle of John, chap. 1. v. 9. *If we confess our sins, God is faithful and just to forgive us our sins, and to cleanse us from all unrighteousness.* This was a precious time to me. While you were preaching, a divine light shone in upon my heart with the word, and I was clearly convinced of the doctrine of sanctification, and the attainableness of it. I came home with full purpose of heart, not to rest till I was made a living witness of it. I had now a clear view. 1. Of the holiness of God, and saw that sin could not dwell with him. 2. I had a clear view of the purity and perfection of his law, which is a transcript of the divine nature. And 3. I felt my great unlikeness to both: and although I felt no condemnation; yet, in the view of these things, I felt much pain in my spirit, and my soul was humbled in the dust before him! Oh! how I longed to be made like him, and to love him with all my heart, soul, mind, and strength. I had glorious discoveries of the grand provision made in the new-covenant, for the complete salvation of the soul: and I went on in joyful expectation, crying to the Lord to put me in possession of all he had purchased for me, and promised to me; sometimes I seemed to be upon the threshold, just stepping into glorious liberty: but again fear and unbelief prevailed, and I started back. This cast my mind into great perplexity, and I often reasoned concerning the truth of the thing.

It would be tedious to relate the various exercises I went through for several years, without opening my mind to any one. I do not remember, that I ever conversed with one upon the subject, or ever heard any one discourse upon it. Only, I think about eighteen years ago, it pleased God that I heard Mr. Olivers preach a sermon upon the subject. His text was, *Let us go on unto perfection.* His doctrine was clear, and his arguments strong. My heart consented to the whole truth, and I had clearer views of the way of attaining it, namely, by faith, than ever before. This added new vigor to my spirit, and I seemed to be more on the wing than ever. I prayed and wept at his footstool, that he would shew me all his salvation. And he gave me to experience such a measure of his grace, as I never knew before: a great measure of heavenly light and divine power spread through all my soul: I found unbelief taken away out of my heart: my soul was filled with such faith as I never felt before: my love to Christ was like fire, and I had such views of him, as my life, my portion, my all, as swallowed me up; and oh! how I longed to be with him! A change passed upon all the powers of my soul, and I felt a great increase of holy and heavenly tempers. I may say, with humility, it was as though I was emptied of all evil, and filled with heaven and God.

Thus, under the influence of his power and grace, I rode upon the sky. My soul fed on angels' food, and I truly ate the bread of heaven. I had more glorious discoveries than ever of the gospel of God our Savior, and especially in his saving the soul from all sin. I enjoyed such an evidence of this in my own mind as put me beyond all doubt; and yet I never had such a sense of my own littleness, helplessness, and unworthiness as now. So true it is, that only grace can humble the soul! From the time the Lord gave me to experience this grace, I became an advocate for the glorious doctrine of Christian perfection. According to the gift he has been pleased to give me, I bear a testimony of it wherever I go and I never find my soul so happy as when I preach most upon the blessed subject.

Thus I have simply related what I know of the work of God in my heart. I desire to give him all the glory. But I have great cause to be ashamed before him for my unfaithfulness. I feel the need of his grace every moment. I stand by faith, and have as much need of Christ as ever: I may truly say,

"Every moment, Lord, I want
The merit of thy death."

Glory be to his name, I find my soul united to him, and my heart cries, None but Christ! I am kept by his power: I enjoy salvation: my heart is fixed, my anchor is sure and steadfast: I believe nothing shall separate me from the love of God, which is in Christ Jesus. I conclude with saying though the whole of our salvation is from the Lord, yet he deals with us as rational creatures. He gives us light and conviction of our lost state; then the heart is humbled, and the soul bows before him. He then speaks peace. This is done in a moment, and faith in the soul is the instrumental root of all Christian holiness. Thus the work of sanctification is begun in the heart, and the person is in a capacity of living to God, and growing in grace. If he finds us faithful in a little, he shews us there is a state of greater liberty provided for us. The soul being open to the divine teaching, he shews us our want of this. We seek it with our whole heart, and he is pleased to put us in possession of it. This too is generally given in a moment, and perfectly frees the mind from all evil tempers, and enables us to *love the Lord with all our hearts, and our neighbors as ourselves.* Being thus perfected in love, we are much more qualified to grow in grace, and in the knowledge of our Lord and Savior Jesus Christ, than ever. O precious salvation! let me ever be a witness of it!   W. H.

THE EXPERIENCE OF REV. ROBT. WILK-INSON.

Before hearing the Gospel, which is the power of God unto salvation, I was often terrified in dreams and visions of the night. Sometimes I thought I was falling down steep precipices; at others, that the devil was standing over me to take me away immediately. At such times, I have often awakened, shrieking in such a manner as terrified all who heard me. Afterwards I heard the gospel for a season, at Rookhope, in the county of Durham; but the people not receiving the joyful sound, the servants of God forsook the place. I was left with much uneasiness on my mind; what I formerly delighted in, was now hateful to me. I could play no more on the violin, or at cards, nor sing vain songs; neither had I a desire to speak any more than I was forced to. The people saw my distress, but not knowing God, could not point out a cure. In this condition I continued for some weeks. I began to read religious books, and likewise to bow my knees before God in secret; sometimes I could weep much, but having no one to direct me, after a time I got back into folly, and pursued my evil practices with more eagerness than before. About four years after, I was called to live in Weardale chapel. I then heard the Methodists very frequently. I was often softened under the word. I never found a desire to mock the people as many do; but rather stood in awe of them. But all this while I continued in my sins. The first Sunday in Lent, 1767, I heard, as usual, a Methodist preacher in the afternoon. I did not then find that the word made any impression upon me. But at night, on my bed, the Lord cut me to the heart, and I could not help roaring for the disquietness of my soul. I then felt I must perish eternally, unless some way to escape were found which I knew not of. Immediately I wished for the Methodists to pray with me; but in particular for a young man, Stephen Watson, who is now in glory. [From the time he knew Jesus, he was a pattern to all the society. And after having walked four years in the light of God's countenance, he departed in the full assurance of faith; having testified for many months before his death, that the blood of Jesus had cleansed him from all sin. His last words were, "Glory be to God for ever and ever! Amen and Amen!"]

One morning I fell down on my knees to ask forgiveness for my many offences, and continued to cry night and day. My burden increased, and temptations were very strong. I then began to compare myself with the most sinful of my companions, and with other notorious sinners I had heard of; but I could find no equal. I said, from the ground of my heart, of all the sinners under heaven, I am the chief. The enemy then suggested, that I was guilty of a sin which God never would pardon. Tongue cannot express the distress I then felt. The heart knoweth its own bitterness. I thought, never man suffered what I did. That saying, "A dreadful sound in his ears," continually followed me. I found the enemy ready day and night to devour me. When in private prayer, I thought he had hold of my clothes. For many nights he suggested, if I prayed, he would appear and tear me in pieces. Yet I durst not but pray, though my prayers were mostly made up of sighs and groans. One day, drawing towards evening, the enemy came in as a flood, and the temptation was, to put an end to a wretched life. I resisted, but it continued to come as quick as lightning, and I was afraid that the tempter would prevail, so that I durst not carry a penknife about me. That was the only time I was banished from private prayer, because I durst not stay alone. That night we met our class; I then cried out to one of my brethren, who was waiting for me to go with him to the meeting, O Cuthbert! I am driven to distraction! He spake to me as comfortably as he could; but as we walked together, I felt as if one was hanging on the skirts of my clothes. After the first prayer was over, it was with difficulty I rose from my knees. When the leader asked how I found the state of my soul, I answered, I am left without one spark of hope that God will ever have mercy on me. No, said he, you are not; for if you were, you would not now be using the means of grace. He encouraged me to follow on; but I still found no comfort. All the time of my convictions I had but very little ease, and when I had, I had a fear almost equal to my pain, lest I should fall back into sin, or speak peace when God did not. O how I longed for deliverance from sin! I often cried, Lord, if I am for ever banished from thy presence, let me not sin again. Not long after, that text in the 51st Psalm followed me, "Then will I teach transgressors thy ways, and sinners shall be converted unto thee." I thought if God did pardon me, he could refuse none; but the foulest on this side hell might come and welcome. But this was the sting, I thought he would not. However, I kept using the means and went frequently among the Methodists, to get them to pray with me. And I would have been glad, if they had asked me to stay all night, but shame would not let me tell them so. I often thought I never could get over another night. My neighbors said, I was beside myself, for I could not rest in my bed. I often rose and wandered in the fields, weeping and bewailing my desperate state. But, blessed be God, he that wounds can heal.

In the beginning of July, as Stephen Watson and I were sitting together, he had a volume of the Christian library in his hand, out of which he read one of Mr. Rutherford's letters. When he had done, Stephen, said I, I find as it were a melting warmness in my breast. So do I, said he. He then asked, cannot you believe that God has pardoned your sins! No, said I. I dare not; on which I immediately lost my comfort.

Sunday, the 12th of July, Joseph Watson preached in the chapel in Weardale. He gave out that hymn,

All ye that pass by,
To Jesus draw nigh,
To you is it nothing that Jesus should die?
Your ransom and peace,
Your surety he is,
Come, see if there ever was sorrow like his.
For you and for me
He prayed on the tree,

The prayer is accepted, the sinner is free:—
Then, all within me cried out,

> The sinner am I
> Who on Jesus rely,
> And come for the pardon God cannot deny.

I then believed that God, for Christ's sake, had forgiven all my sins, and found that peace which arises from a sense of reconciliation. The people of God who knew my distress, perceived by my countenance that the Lord was gracious to me, before I had the opportunity to tell them. I then went rejoicing home, and could not help telling what God had done for my soul. It was not long before my faith was tried. One of our brethren, a Calvinist, lent me a book. As I read, I thought Mr. Wesley was quite in the wrong; and I found something in me that rose against him: yet one thing I remember I could not swallow, which was, the author asserted that a sense of inbred sin would reconcile us to death. No, said Mr. Wesley, nothing but perfect love. Indeed I could not persuade myself that the sting of death could reconcile us to death itself. However, I read and reasoned myself miserable. Yet the Lord gave me grace to wrestle with him in prayer; and every day I found more or less the witness of my sonship. I was then afraid, if I sought after holiness, I should rob Christ of his glory. Some of our people hearing that I read that book, conversed with the man who lent it, took it for granted that I was prejudiced against the doctrine of perfection and those that preached it. They told this to my band-leader. I went one Sunday morning, as usual, at seven o'clock, to meet my band, and found myself in a peaceable frame of mind. No sooner did the leader begin to pray, than he cried, "Lord, never suffer us to be prejudiced against thy servants, seeing that thy will is our sanctification." I found as it were, something in me saying, he means me. When he spoke his experience, he expressed the same thing; on which I said, It is me you mean. He answered, "What I have said, I have said." I then found violent prejudice against him. My peace was gone. My soul was torn in pieces within me. I told one of our people, as we went home, how my leader had behaved towards me. I did not regard breaking the band rules, because I was determined never to meet in a band any more. I had no rest: though I could not give up my confidence in God; nevertheless my corruptions boiled so within me, that I could have fought with a feather.

On Friday night we had preaching. I went to it like one possessed with a legion of devils. Afterwards the band met, and the preacher earnestly exhorted all present to look for the second blessing, and insisted that it might be received. Now, thought I, if there is such a thing, none can stand in more need of it than I do. But the enemy suggested, "There are those that have known God several years, and have not attained; and shalt thou be delivered who hast been justified only a few months?" Immediately I found power to resist the temptation, and said within myself, God is not tied to time. No sooner did that thought pass through my heart than the power of God seized me. I found I could not resist, and therefore turned myself over upon the seat: I cannot express how I was. I found such a travail in my soul as if it would burst from the body. I continued so, till I was

motionless and insensible for a season. But as I was
coming to myself I found such an emptying, and then
such a heaven of love springing up in my soul, as I
had never felt before: with an application of these
blessed words, "He that believeth on me, as the scripture hath said, out of his belly shall flow rivers of living
water." If possible, I could have put my band-leader
into my heart. The book I mentioned before, had pleased me so well, that I had given orders to him that lent
it me, to buy me one of them. But no sooner did God
work this change in my soul, than I found an utter aver-
sion to it, and told the man, you must not buy it; for
I shall never read it more.

In the year 1768, I was sent to call sinners to repentance, in and about the city of Carlisle. Here I was
much persecuted; but, blessed be God, he delivered me
out of the hands of all my enemies, and gave me several
seals to my ministry.

[*Thus far Mr. Wilkinson lived to write himself. One
of his fellow-laborers added what follows.*]

My acquaintance with Mr. Wilkinson was very short.
The first time I ever saw him was a little above three
years ago. The next time was after last Bristol conference. He was there appointed to labor with me in and
about Grimsby. When we met in the circuit we were
both in health; but the day before our quarterly-meet-
ing, I was taken very ill of a fever; however the next
morning I ventured to set out for the meeting; but having fifteen miles to ride, it was with much difficulty I
got safe thither. And then I was unable to attend either
the love-feast or the watch-night. But I shall never for-

get the prayer Mr. Wilkinson put up for me at the close
of the love-feast, "That the Lord would spare me a little longer, and raise me up again to labor in his vine-
yard." His prayer pierced the heavens, the power of
God came down upon the people like a torrent of rain.
They were so affected that they wept and rejoiced abundantly. Immediately I shared with them, although I
was not in the same room, the divine presence broke my
heart to pieces. My soul overflowed with love, and my
eyes with tears. I know not that I was ever so powerful-
ly and suddenly affected under any person's prayer, ex-
cept on the day I was converted to God. Immediately
I had faith to believe the Lord would raise me up again,
and for several minutes it appeared to me as if I
was perfectly well. The next day I went along with
him to Louth; and in that time we had a good deal of
conversation together, which chiefly turned upon these
two points, viz., Predestination, and Christian Perfection. He told me with sorrow of heart, how often he
had been grieved for the immense hurt that he
had seen done by the preaching of unconditional predestination, as it blocked up the way of repentance;
weakened the foundation of diligence; damped the fervor
of believers after holiness; and had a tendency to destroy
it root and branch. He likewise very warmly expressed
his love for Bible holiness, saying, it was the delight of
his soul to press after it himself, and to enforce it upon
others; and that while he was doing this, the Lord
blessed him most in his labors, and shone clearest upon
the work he had wrought in his own soul. He signified
to me that the Lord had circumcised his heart to love

the Lord his God with all his heart, with all his soul, and with all his strength; and I believe, at that time, he was full of faith and the Holy Ghost.

He was truly meek, and lowly of heart; and little, and mean, and vile in his own eyes. I found my mind amazingly united to him, for the time we were together, like the soul of David and his beloved Jonathan. I loved him much for the mind of Christ I saw in him, and for his zeal for the Lord of hosts. We parted at Louth, and I endeavored, with the fever upon me, to creep along to Tedford to preach: but it was with much trouble I went through my discourse. That night the fever seized upon me more violently, and never left me for near a month. About a week after, Mr. Wilkinson came to Tedford to see me. We spent about three hours together very profitably. We then both of us prayed, and commended each other to God.

A few days after we parted, he was taken ill of the fever, and could not rest until he came to his wife at Grimsby: where he lay ill for four or five weeks. He then appeared to be recovering fast, and walked about a little: but he suddenly relapsed, and was carried off in about a week. He bore all his afflictions with great patience, frequently lifting up his heart to God, and repeating these words: "But he knoweth the way that I take: when he hath tried me, I shall come forth as gold. My foot hath held his steps, his way have I kept, and not declined. Neither have I gone back from the commandments of his lips: I have esteemed the words of his mouth, more than my necessary food." Job. xxiii. When he perceived that he should die, he exhorted his wife to cast all her care upon the Lord: and encouraged her to believe that his grace was sufficient for her. He then prayed for her and his two children: earnestly entreating the Lord to protect them in this troublesome world, and to supply all their wants. He next prayed fervently for Mr. Wesley, that the presence of the Lord might continue with him all his days, and crown him at last with eternal glory. He then remembered his three fellow-laborers in the circuit, praying that the Redeemer would assist us in the great work: that he would go forth with, and bless the labors of all the preachers, and that the kingdom of the Redeemer might spread unto the ends of the earth, and preserve them until they join the church triumphant.

In the night season, he had a severe conflict with Satan, and his spirit wrestled with God in prayer. Yea, he was in an agony, as he said afterwards. At last the tempter fled, and he seemed as if he was admitted into heaven, to converse with God, with angels, and saints. He suddenly waked his wife (who was in the same room) and said, "Thou hast been sleeping, but I have been in heaven. O what has the Lord discovered to me this night! O the glory of God! the glory of God and heaven! the celestial city! the New Jerusalem! O the lovely beauty! the happiness of Paradise! God is all love; he is nothing but love! O, help me to praise him! O, help me to praise him! I shall praise him forever! I shall praise him forever! I shall praise him forever!" So Robert Wilkinson departed this life in peace, on Friday, December 8th, about eleven o'clock, 1780.

It seemed a great Providence that he died on the

market day, when a number of friends out of the country
were present, who quickly published, in their little villages, that a funeral sermon would be preached on Sunday. The house was well filled, and the Lord made it a
solemn time. I believe there was scarcely a dry eye in
the congregation. I have often taken notice, how the
Lord makes the triumphant death of good men a pe-
culiar blessing to his children, who are left behind; so
it was at this time. The people of God were remarkably
blest in hearing the dying testimony of our dear friend.
The worldly people and the backsliders also were cut to
the heart. At the conclusion of the sermon I dropped
these words: Earth has lost, and heaven has gained a
child of God. Let us pray the Lord to add another to the
church militant. We did so; and the Lord answered our
prayer, by setting a young man's soul at liberty, so that
he went from the solemn place, as the shepherds from
the heavenly vision, blessing, praising, and glorifying
God.

The minister of the parish behaved exceeding kind;
he came to the preaching-house, stayed awhile, and then
walked slowly before the corpse; whilst the people sung
a hymn of praise. When we arrived at the church, one
of our friends asked him if we might sing a hymn. He
answered, "I have no objection; I am against nothing
that is good," so we sung those awful words,

> "Thee we adore, eternal name,
>   And humbly own to thee,
> How feeble is our mortal frame,
>   What dying worms we be!"

The people sang lustily and with a solemn spirit; for

the divine presence was with us all the way through; and in such a manner as I never knew before at any funeral. When the minister read these words, "Not to be sorry as men without hope," Mrs. Wilkinson (who hung upon my arm with her two little babes) was so overwhelmed with the presence of God, that she could not refrain from crying out, "Sorry! no! Glory be to God! glory be to God! Glory, and praise and blessing, be ascribed unto God, for ever, and ever!" Her spirit seemed as if it was ready to launch into the eternal world, to be with Jesus and her happy husband. A remarkable power fell on all that could hear her; so that the people were melted into tears; some of sorrow, others of joy.

From this time the work of God began to revive at Brimsby, and the country people caught the fire, and carried it along with them into their little societies.

Robert Wilkinson was, as you have described him, "An Israelite indeed, a man of faith and prayer: who, having been a pattern of all good works, died in the full triumph of faith." O what a blessing to live and die a Christian! May I also be a follower of those who through faith and patience inherit the promises! In my life, and at my death, may I be like him.

LEAVES FROM THE TREE OF LIFE.

REV. L. L. PICKETT.

CLOTH, $1.00.

Th's is a book of 76 Bible readings on various subjects. We have such questions as the following: "Apostasy," "How to Prevent Apostasy," "Missions," Christian Giving," Consecration," "Holiness," "Entire Sanctification," "Woman's Ministry," etc. The Bible lessons in this issue of Bible Truth Library are from this book. It is commended in strong terms and has proven very helpful to many souls. Let the reader get it.

Other Books by the Same Author.

The Book and Its Theme.................. ....cloth	$1	00
The Theme of The Book......................paper		50
The Book or The Inspiration of the Scriptures..paper		15
The Danger Signal, or a Shot at the Foe...........	1	00
Bible Fruit......... ....paper 50 cts., cloth	1	00
The Blessed Hope...... ....cloth $1.00 and	1	25
The Holy Day or Remember the Sabbath........ ...		10
Saint Paul on Holiness............................		05
Pickett-Smith Debate on Sanctification........ ..	1	00
paper	_	50
A Plea for the Holiness Movement........ . paper		15
cloth		25
Our King Cometh................... paper 10, cloth		25
Why I Do Not Immerse............................		10
Holiness. Doctrine, Experience, Practice, paper....		25
cloth		35

Pickett Publishing Co.
Louisville, Ky.

www.ingramcontent.com/pod-product-compliance
Lightning Source LLC
Chambersburg PA
CBHW020511030426
42337CB00011B/330